c-mail

Being a Christian –
your questions answered

- stories
- sketches
- readings

Tony Bower

kevin
mayhew

First published in 2002 by
KEVIN MAYHEW LTD
Buxhall, Stowmarket, Suffolk IP14 3BW
E-mail: info@kevinmayhewltd.com

9 8 7 6 5 4 3 2 1 0

ISBN 1 84003 903 5
Catalogue number 1500500

Cover design by Angela Selfe
Edited and typeset by Elisabeth Bates
Printed in Great Britain

Contents

About the author

Tony Bower is married to Claire and they have a son, Joseph. Tony is a full-time Christian Schools Worker for NISCU (Northern Inter-schools Christian Union). He is also one of the writing team for Scripture Union's SALT magazine for 11-14s, and author of *Buried Treasure* and *The Word That Changed the World*, Christian drama books (Kevin Mayhew).

Tony is also an outstanding international footballer and test cricketer, but only in his dreams!

A word of thanks

To the Hepworth family, Dennis Bavister, Ian Taylor and all those who helped answer my questions as a young Christian. To Kate Lewis and Debbie Green without whom *C-mail* would not have been possible.

Introduction

C-mail is a discipleship course for young people who are new to Christianity. If you are a young person reading this book you can read it in a number of ways:

- Read straight through as a book to enjoy.
- Read and do a personal study at the end of each unit.
- Read and do the study, then use the questions for an older Christian to help you with. You could discuss them with friends or use it in a study group.

Alternatively, the book can be used within a group context such as a Christian Union or youth group, with the question-and-answer pages being given to the leader after each session.

Each unit will hopefully give some answers but also be a stimulus. I pray that the book will both answer some of your questions and encourage you to dig deeper in your faith.

Unit 1

Creation

Dear Jake,

Hello, it's Sam — you probably don't remember me. I was the one who put a custard pie in your face the last night of camp. I also became a Christian that night. Do you remember? It was you I talked to. You gave me lots of really good advice. Thing is, I've forgotten what you said.

Now school's started, camp seems years ago. None of my mates at school are Christians, and I haven't got round to telling them yet, but I will. I do remember you telling me I could write to you if I needed any help, and you would try and sort it. Well, thing is, I know I said I wanted to be a Christian, and I still do, but I'm not really sure about lots of stuff — like who is God? What's he like? No one's ever seen him, have they? Did he really make the world and everyone in it?

So, I was wondering if you could help me out. I tried asking my mum and dad, but they said I was just going through a phase, and I'd soon get over it. When I came home from camp and started reading my Bible, every time Dad saw me, he kept singing, 'Hallelujah praise the Lord' and then started laughing. I don't read my Bible downstairs now.

Mum's alright about it really, she doesn't make fun, just says, 'As long as you've done your homework' and things like that. My brother's the worst; he's 2 years older than me and thinks he knows everything. He keeps calling me Vic just 'cos he knows it annoys me. He also keeps threatening to tell all my mates I've gone all religious. Not that I'm bothered like, but he does annoy me.

Got to go now, Mum's shouting it's time for tea. Hope you remember me. Hope you're not too busy to write.

See ya,

Sam

PS Which football team do you support?

Dear Sam,

Thanks for your letter. It was great to hear from you, and yes, I do remember you. I will never forget. I spent ages trying to get that custard pie mix off my face and my clothes! Thanks!! I'll never forget you telling me you wanted to become a Christian. That was so great. I've never seen as big a grin as you had on your face. You were still grinning from ear to ear when you climbed on the bus the next day.

Sounds like your family aren't quite sure what to make of things. My parents were exactly the same when I became a Christian, a long time ago now. When they see that you're not into something weird or dangerous they'll be OK. When they see what a positive difference Christianity is making in your life they'll be over the moon. God only changes people for the better and he always does us good. He will never let us down, never disappoint us and never leave us.

Sorry Sam, I'm slipping into preaching mode; occupational hazard I'm afraid. You probably heard enough of me spouting on at camp! I will, however, try to answer your questions.

Who is God? What is he like? Big questions. I've been running a course recently on 'Christianity for Beginners'. Not a fancy title, I know, but it's for people like yourself who have just become Christians. I've adapted the course notes and enclosed them for you to read. I hope you find them helpful. If they're too long-winded, too boring, or whatever, please let me know. I really want to try to help and answer your questions.

Bye for now,

Jake

PS I support the Super-Reds!

Checking for fingerprints

Scene
A man holding his head in his hands. He is very distraught. Taking away his hands, he looks around the room, shaking his head. There is a knock at the door.

Characters
Man (M); Detective Inspector (DI)

M Hello, who are you?

The man at the door flashes his ID card

DI Detective Inspector Plonker of the Yard.

M Scotland Yard?

DI No, Sir, this is England.

The DI enters the room

DI How can we be of service, Sir?

M You can catch the person who did all this.

The man waves his arm around the room

DI Did what, Sir?

M Did this!

DI What exactly is this, Sir?

The man is now becoming a little exasperated

M This!

As the man says 'this', he opens his arms wide. The DI nods as if in understanding

DI: Aah, this . . .

When the DI says this, he opens his arms wide, copying the man, but still completely clueless. The man is now extremely exasperated

M Not this *(Opens his arms out)*. This! *(Shows him the room)*

DI Oh, you mean all this mess.

M Exactly.

DI Sorry, Sir. I didn't want to be rude. Some people like to live a little untidily.

M A little untidily! A little untidily! The house has been ransacked! Broken into, vandalised, wrecked, destroyed. It looks like a bomb's hit it!

The DI has a good look around

DI I must admit, Sir, when I stepped through the door, I thought 'ello, 'ello, 'ello.

M And . . .

DI And what, Sir?

M What did you think?

DI I just said, Sir.

M Said what?

DI 'Ello, 'ello, 'ello.

M That's all you thought?

DI Yes, Sir.

M What about the house?

DI looks around the house

DI It does look a little untidy, Sir. Not meaning to be critical, Sir.

M Untidy? Untidy? I have been burgled, broken into. My house is in a complete mess.

DI Really, Sir?

M Look at the window!

DI You must be careful near windows, Sir.

M Careful near windows? What on earth are you on about?

DI Looks like you've dropped a brick on it.

M Dropped a brick on it? Someone threw a brick through the window.

DI Oh dear, Sir.

M Oh dear?

DI That was very careless.

M Careless?

DI Throwing bricks so close to glass. It can lead to nasty accidents.

M Accidents? What are you on about? I have been burgled. The thief threw the brick through the window. The thief stole all my possessions. The thief wrote graffiti on the walls. The thief poured paint on the carpet. The thief wrote me a message:

> Ha ha! Hee hee! Try as you may,
> you'll never catch me.
> Love, The Burglar

DI That is very careless.

M Careless? What's careless?

DI Painting without a dustsheet. You've made lots of spills on the carpet.

M I don't believe I'm hearing this! Are you a complete plonker?

DI I do answer to that name, Sir.

M Why don't you look at the evidence. Why don't you dust for fingerprints?

DI My recommendation, Sir . . .

M Yes?

DI . . . next time you have a bit of a party, make sure you clean up afterwards.

M Party? Party? Can't you see with your eyes that someone's been here? Can't you see the thief's note? Are you a total plonker?

DI Yes, Sir, I am. Detective Inspector Plonker of the Yard.

M But not Scotland Yard . . .

DI Don't be silly, Sir. We're in England. Good day, Sir. Glad to be of service.

He exits, leaving the man in shock

The DI didn't bother checking for fingerprints because he failed to recognise any signs of a burglary! This situation could never happen because no one could be that foolish.

In a magazine I read recently I came across the phrase 'God's fingerprints are all over creation'. It's true. There is evidence of the creator God everywhere, if only people would open their eyes and see. Let's take a look at the evidence . . .

The Big Bang: Evolution or maybe something a little more organised?

- How did our world come into being?
- How did the human race evolve?
- How big is the universe?
- How come we want to know the answers to such questions?
- How come cheese and onion crisps are the best flavour?

Life is full of big, tough questions. Questions that have been asked and pondered upon by each generation. Why are we here on planet earth? Is it by some almighty, cosmic fluke, or is it by some almighty Creator? Mishap or Maker? Default or design? The choice is between these two camps. There cannot be a third alternative, neither can there be a mix of the two camps. Either someone, God, made this world, this universe, including us, or by some freak of nature our planet formed out of some kind of gigantic explosion in deepest space. Spinning in orbit around a glowing ball called the sun, this wonderful accident gave life to every species now appearing on this earth, including humankind. Humankind who constantly asks those deep, searching questions – Why are we here? How did we get to be here?

What do you believe? I find it difficult to believe that this wonderful world, held in perfect harmony, 'just happened'. It is like believing that you could blow up a tower block and find that as the bricks fall to earth they assemble into a huge palace, fit for a King. Each room perfectly laid out and fitted. Every detail perfected. Why are you laughing? Why do you find this so hard to believe? This is nothing to believing that our entire universe simply 'happened'.

Charles Darwin wrote: 'To suppose that the eye, with so many parts all working together, could have been formed by natural selection, seems, I freely confess, absurd in the highest degree'.

Scientists have been trying to produce a camera with the sophistication of the human eye for years and still fall short. The eye can regulate the amount of light entering by stretching the soft lens and then receives the image on a small panel containing 150,000,000 light receptors, each capable of processing millions of tiny light energy particles entering every second.

Sounds pretty amazing to me! Sounds absolutely fantastic! That is only one part of our incredible bodies. How could that have simply just happened? Even Charles Darwin didn't believe it could have just happened or evolved!

When my son was six weeks old in his mother's womb, I saw him. I could see him on a scan. He didn't look like a human being, more like a jelly baby. He was so tiny and yet we could see his heart beat and we could see him moving. When he was about eighteen weeks old I saw him again on the scan. Wow! How he had grown. This time I could see his head, his back, his legs, his arms: my son. I could have sat there watching him all day, but I think the doctor had other appointments!

The next time I saw him was when he was born. In those first few seconds of his life, when the midwife picked him up I could see him. I could hear him. He was testing his lungs and they were in perfect working order! It is hard to describe that moment or to convey the feelings I had, the sense of awe and wonder. One word, perhaps, can do justice: MIRACLE!

People will pay millions of pounds to gain possession of a masterpiece. Why? Because they value masterpieces so much; they are originals and there aren't others like them, nor will there ever be.

I praise you because I am fearfully and wonderfully made; your works are wonderful. Psalm 139:14

The Bible teaches that we are all masterpieces created by God. We are unique individuals and we are highly valued. Valued so highly in fact that God was prepared to let Jesus Christ, his Son, die to give us forgiveness and a way to know him again.

Before I formed you in the womb, I knew you. Jeremiah 1:5

I made the mountains,
I made you.
I made the oceans,
I made you.
I made the valleys,
I made you.
I made the lion roar,
I made you.
I made the caterpillar change,
I made you.

God looked at all that he had made
and said that it was good.

By the way, that includes you.

Read Genesis chapter 1 and Psalm 139

Q Why do you think God created man?
A

Q What does Genesis chapter 1 teach us about God?
A

Q How does Psalm 139 make you feel?
A

Q What does Psalm 139 teach us about God?
A

Q When did God first know us?
A

Any comments on what you've read:

Any questions you'd like to ask:

Unit 2

God our Father

Dear Jake,

Hi! Thanks for your letter. I'm glad you wrote to me. I didn't think you would. I didn't think you'd remember me. Thanks anyway. I hope you don't mind me writing again but I'm a bit confused about some stuff, and I've no one who can help me.

I'm a bit unsure what God is like. I mean, it's not as if you can see him, is it? Or can you? Perhaps if you are really super-spiritual like you are, then you do get to see him. Does that sound stupid? Only, I am really baffled. I tried asking my dad the other day, but he just gave me a hard time. All he said was, 'Hallelujah! Praise the Lord! Amen!'

After that, I tried asking my mum, but she said she'd talk later when she wasn't so busy. Trouble is, she's always busy, so we never get to talk. I even thought about asking my brother, until he came into the living room and knelt down in front of me. He put his hands together and said, 'Brother, I have something to confess.' He told me that he'd accidentally broken my CD. How can you break a CD? How can you break one accidentally?

I don't know if it's wrong to hit someone while they're down on their knees, but I took a swing at him. I never hit him mind you — he was too quick. Then he said, 'Oh brother, where is your Christian charity? Can you not find it in your soul to forgive such a wretched sinner as me?' I threw a cushion at him. After that incident, I decided not to ask him any questions about God or Christianity. So if my family can't give me an answer, can you?

Write soon,

Sam

PS I didn't know you were a Man U. fan!

Dear Sam,

Thanks for your letter. It was good to hear from you and in answer to your question, no, I don't mind you writing to me and asking me questions. I'm not sure if my answers will be very good, but I'll do my best.

I was speaking at a youth event last week and I was talking about God, our Father, because that is the best picture of what God is like. (By the way, I am not super-spiritual at all and no one can actually see God physically.) Jesus referred to God as our Heavenly Father. One of the greatest stories Jesus ever told was about a father and a son. He shared this parable (story) to illustrate how much God loves us and how much we need him in our lives. I have enclosed my notes that I spoke from. I hope it's not too long and boring. I hope it will give you some understanding of who God really is. I have put a few comments at the bottom of my notes for you. I hope you find these helpful.

Yours sincerely,

Jake

PS I am not a Man U. fan. I support THE Super-Reds!

A story of three sons . . .

Some mothers do 'ave 'em!

Let me share with you a story about a young man.

This boy was so selfish that he would scream in the shops in town when he was with his mother. Scream and point furiously at the toys he wanted, scream until his demands were met. This boy was so selfish that he manipulated his mother when he had his arm in a sling. He pretended he was in agony, and showed her his big blue eyes; he looked longingly at the toys on the shelves until his mother bought them for him. That selfish boy grew up and continued his selfish acts. That boy is me!

That is my story. If we are all honest we can all identify with the young man in the story. We are, by nature, selfish. We have a wrong, self-centred heart that needs dealing with, but more of that later. We may not have broken the law of the land but we have all broken God's laws. We have all been guilty of going our own way, of ignoring God and of ignoring others.

How should we respond to our problem? How can we put our relationship right with God? What is God's response to us? Let's look at a classic, timeless story that answers those basic questions.

Lost and found

An everyday story of everyday life . . .

A young man demands and receives his inheritance from his father. Having acquired his worldly wealth he goes off to a distant country and squanders it all in wild living. A famine hits the land; with his pockets empty and desperate for food he finds work on a pig farm where he has to do daily battle with the animals to eat their left-overs.

One day the young man wakes up and comes to his senses. He realises what he is missing: his home, his father. He decides it's time to go home and begins to prepare himself for the journey. He no longer considers himself worthy to be called a son. Once he demanded his inheritance, now he will settle for a place in the servants' quarters. Once he dared approach his father for every penny possible, now he daren't even look in his father's face, let alone look into his eyes.

A biblical word to describe the transformation in the young man's heart is 'repentance'. The realisation that you are in the wrong, the need to turn back to the God who made you and to throw yourself at his mercy, knowing that you deserve nothing, but knowing there is nowhere else to go, no other hope.

We can never come to God on our terms, we can only go to him on his. We must realise what an appalling condition we are in as we bow our hearts and our knees before him. Will he, could he, possibly take us back into the family home after all our reckless living?

These thoughts tumbled through the mind of this young man as he wearily approached his father's house. With his head dropped, his speech rehearsed and not far from home, he wondered in his heart if he would ever be welcomed in, let alone accepted and loved.

What was the greeting he received? What was the Father's response? How did the father react when he saw his wayward son wearily walking his way home? Did he wait on the front doorstep to pour his anger and frustration out upon his son? Did he stand with his arms folded? Did he stand with the keys to the 'dog-house' in his hand?

NO! He did not stand at all. He could not stand waiting any longer. He had waited so long for this moment, the moment he might see his beloved son returning home where he belonged. The waiting was over. Without losing a moment, he left the house, went down the garden path and across the fields running like the wind to greet his son, tears of joy streaming down his cheeks as he saw the child he loved standing before him. Before he heard the young man's speech, his arms of love had embraced his son. He saw his rags and gave him a robe. He saw his bony, wasted fingers and put on a ring. He saw his hunger and ordered the feast to begin. He saw his son, who he thought was dead but was now alive. He saw his son who once was lost, but now was found.

Maybe you struggle with this story, with the picture of a loving father. Perhaps your own father has not displayed the kind of love you need. God is our perfect, heavenly Father. He is consistent in his caring. He is true to his word. He is a faithful father. He is always there for us and he always, always cares for us.

Chariots without wheels

There is a true story about a British athlete called Derek Redmond. He managed to make it to the finals in an Olympic event. He was in the finest form of his life. He had every chance of winning a medal. Maybe, if he ran the race of his life, the coveted Gold itself.

Inside a packed stadium of thousands, watched world-wide by millions, the race began. Derek Redmond ran like the wind, the crowd cheered and roared as the athletes raced towards the tape. Before the tape was broken something else snapped! Something in Derek Redmond's leg. In an instant he fell to the ground and lay in a crumpled heap. As he lay in agony on the track he could see the winner cross the line. He watched as every competitor finished the race. Tears began to roll. Not because of his broken body but because of his broken dreams. All of his life's ambitions were cruelly snatched from him in that instant of sheer pain that shot through his leg.

The cheers from the crowd subsided and all attention shifted. Eyes that had been fixed on the winner now focused on Derek Redmond. Getting to his feet and clutching hold of his leg he bravely moved forward towards the finish. Silence fell amongst the thousands watching, observing this one man's attempt to finish the race.

Out of the crowd a man appeared. He dodged the stewards who tried to restrain him and ran on to the track. Reaching Derek Redmond, he flung his arms around him, only to be shoved away. Derek Redmond did not want any-body's help. It was his race. The man tried again, putting his arms around the athlete. This time, Derek Redmond turned to face the man. Only this time he didn't push him away, he just stared at him. The man put his arms out to support Derek Redmond and the two men began their walk towards the line. Slow, painful steps, with tears streaming down the cheeks of these two men. They crossed the line together. They finished the race embracing one another. Father and son. Derek Redmond's father couldn't bear to see his son's struggle, his son in pain. He had to do something about it. He had to come and help him. He had to be there for him.

This is a wonderful picture of our heavenly father. He doesn't want to sit in the stands, watching our struggles. He wants to be there alongside us, helping us every step of the way. Helping us all the way back home.

The choice is ours. Are we going to accept or reject the father's love? He's reached out his arms to us. He's had them nailed to a cross to demonstrate his great love for us. Are we going to allow him to love us as our heavenly father?

Those were the notes for my talk. Like I said, I hope it wasn't too long or boring. I hope it's given you a little more understanding of who God is.

If you read the story in Luke's Gospel you will notice the reaction of the older brother. He is none too pleased with his brother, to put it mildly. Sometimes family life can be fraught with tensions and misunderstandings. We do need to be patient with each other. You never know, one day they may invite _us_ to _their_ party.

Read Luke 15:11-31

Q Why do you think the father gave the son his inheritance?
A

Q Why did the son decide to return home?
A

Q What was the son's attitude?
A

Q What was the father's response?
A

Q What does that teach us about God?
A

Any comments on what you've read:

Any questions you'd like to ask:

Unit 3

What about suffering?

Dear Jake,

Thanks for your letter and all your notes. Did you really scream in the shops? You tinker! I would never have thought you capable of such behaviour. Oh my, oh my!

The story of the Prodigal Son is an amazing one – I've never read it before, and I really enjoyed it. I can't imagine my dad running to greet me if I'd spent all his money (God's something special, isn't he?) The other day we were sitting watching TV and the news came on. Normally that's a signal for me to disappear and go on the computer. Only this time I decided to stay and watch with my dad. He always watches TV. Anyway, the He always watches the news. headlines were all about some civil war going on and all the suffering in that country because of the fighting and the famine. All of a sudden my dad turned to me and started having a go at me. Verbal ear-bashing or what? He went on and on, well, just to give you an idea of what he was going on about, this is roughly how the conversation went.

Dad: It's all his fault, this lot.

Me: Whose fault?

Dad: That God of yours. Him you believe in.

Me: Eh?

Dad: Look at it. Look!

(Dad pointed to the TV screen and I had a good look. There were horrible pictures of people suffering.)

Me: You can't blame God for that.

Dad: Why not?

Me: 'Cos you can't, that's why.

Dad: Says who? If it's his world, he's to blame.

Me: No, he's not.

Dad: Don't be daft, of course it's his fault. That's if he even exists, which I doubt when I look at pictures like that.

Dad pointed to the TV screen again. I didn't know what to say. I knew Dad was wrong, or at least hoped he was wrong, but I didn't have any answers for him. I stood up, grunted loudly in his direction, walked out of the room and slammed the door behind me. It made the house shake. Dad didn't half shout at me, but I just bolted upstairs. I was annoyed, I was upset, but I just couldn't figure it out.

Jake, can you help please? Why is there suffering? Is God to blame? Hope you've got the answers.

Write soon,

Sam

PS I nearly forgot! You must be a Liverpool fan, right?

Dear Sam,

Thanks for your letter. It was good to hear from you again although I'm sorry to hear about your argument with your dad. The question of suffering is one of the biggest questions raised whenever Christianity is mentioned. If we live in a world that God has made and if God is good and he loves us, then why do we see so much pain in the world? So many people suffering? Make no mistake about it, there are major heartaches in the world. So, where is God, and what's he doing about it? Once again I have adapted the notes from my course 'Christianity for Beginners'. I do hope they help answer the question.

Yours sincerely,

Jake

PS I don't support Liverpool. I support THE Super-Reds!!!

Freedom, free choice and a free fall for everyone!

What would you have done? How would you have made it? If you could have been on hand to give advice, what pearls of wisdom would you have offered? How would you have designed the world? A green sky perhaps? A red ocean? Blue grass? Mole hills as big as mountains? Mountains as small as mole hills? I hope we are all agreed. God did a good job. God did a very good job. In the first book of the Bible, Genesis, it tells the story of God creating the world. He looked at all he had made and said that it was good. An understatement if ever there was one. We do live in a beautiful, amazing world. Think of the colours, the animals, the country-side, the countries. What richness, what variety! Yet God's masterpiece was still waiting to be painted upon the canvass of Life: Humankind.

You and I are the ones described as the apple of God's eye. Not the eagle or the elephant, not the sunrise or the seas, not the rainbow or the rivers. No! In the whole of creation we were the ones set apart to have a unique relationship with God and play a special part in his creation.

It was God who set us apart to rule over the world and the animals that dwelt within it. It was God who set us apart to have a personal relationship with him. What a privilege. What an honour. To know the God who made you and to rule over the rest of his creation. Sounds like paradise. Well it was in the Garden of Eden. So, with everything so good, and with everything going for us, what went wrong?

Freedom and free will

When God made us he didn't program us. We are not some highly sophisticated computer game that God is playing. He didn't create us to control us. He made us because he loves us and he wants us to love him. A love which is in response to his love, not because the micro-chip in our electronically controlled brain tells us to. God made us as human beings with flesh and blood, with the capacity to think, to reason and to react. We are free to choose. God gave us free will. A precious gift, but with perilous consequences if we make the wrong choices. God only wants the very best for us. Look at the world as a reminder. Look at the gift of life we possess to drive the point home. The first people who ever walked this planet knew the reality of God's goodness. A beautiful place to live. Companionship with one another and a personal relationship with God. Nothing could go wrong, if they lived in the good of all God had given them. There was only one thing God had told them not to do. One tree in all of the garden that they must not eat from. The rest was theirs to enjoy. With such an idyllic situation, how could paradise become poisoned?

As the story unfolds in Genesis chapter three, we find Eve confronted by a slippery character called the Serpent. He poses the questions which begin to turn in Eve's mind. He leads her down the path of temptation. A path which once taken will lead out of the garden gate.

Adam and Eve ignore God. They ignore God's instructions. They ignore the consequences of their actions and they eat the fruit that was forbidden. Notice that God did not stop them eating. He did not overrule their freedom and free choice, but he did act upon their actions.

Free fall for everyone

Adam and Eve not only determined their own futures but also the destiny of humankind. As they fell from God's grace and goodness, so too they passed the seed on to the rest of the human race. We are all born into Adam, the Bible says. To understand a little more clearly, we inherit his genes, his lineage, and therefore the consequences of his actions. Perhaps you feel aggrieved at your ancestor Adam. If it wasn't for him we would still be playing in Paradise. Before you begin to point the finger, here is a sketch to ponder . . .

Blame it on . . .

Scene

There is a sound of breaking glass, a garden gate is opened, footsteps along the path and a knock on a door.

Woman	Yes?
Boy	Nice day?
Woman	It was.
Boy	Can I have it back now?
Woman	What?
Boy	I think it's in your front room.
Woman	There are lots of things in my front room now.
Boy	All I want is my ball back.
Woman	Ah! So you admit it?
Boy	Admit what?
Woman	That it was your ball that came hurtling through the window at precisely 2.52pm, smashing the glass to smithereens!
Boy	My dad bought me that ball. Can I have it back now?
Woman	Isn't there something you have to say?
Boy	Umm . . . I don't think so . . .
Woman	Think.
Boy	But I only want . . .
Woman	Think!
Boy	Err . . . Oh yeah! *Please* can I have my ball back?
Woman	No.
Boy	But it's my ball.
Woman	But it's in my front room.
Boy	But it belongs to me.
Woman	Oh. You can have it back.
Boy	Good.

Woman	When you say the word.
Boy	What word?
Woman	Are you trying to tell me that you don't know what I'm talking about?
Boy	Yeah.
Woman	Let me try to help you understand. Who kicked the ball that flew into my house via the pane of glass in my window?
Boy	I did.
Woman	I am glad that we have established that fact. So what do you say?
Boy	It wasn't my fault.
Woman	It wasn't your fault?
Boy	No. It was the keeper's. He should have saved my shot easily but he's rubbish, he's useless. He couldn't even catch a cold, never mind a football!
Woman	Did you hit the ball straight at the goal keeper?
Boy	No. Of course not! I was trying to score a goal.
Woman	So would you say that you cracked the ball as hard as you could?
Boy	Smashed it right into the top corner. Keeper didn't have a ch . . . It's my trainers.
Woman	Your trainers?
Boy	Cost my mum and dad a fortune, they did. It's their fault.
Woman	Their fault?
Boy	Yeah.
Woman	It was their fault? The people who made your training shoes?
Boy	Yeah. They shouldn't have made them so good.
Woman	So, this afternoon your training shoes ran out of your house, single-footedly dribbled around all of the defenders and shot the ball into the goal without any human aid or effort?
Boy	Don't be so sil . . . It's Ryan Giggs' fault.
Woman	Ryan Giggs?
Boy	Yeah. If Ryan Giggs hadn't invented football, then I wouldn't have been playing football outside your window.

Woman Ryan Giggs did not invent football.
Boy He didn't?
Woman No.
Boy It's not his fault, then, either.
Woman So what do you say then?
Boy Can I have my ball back . . . PLEASE!!!

Mirrors

House of fun, filled with mirrors.
Look at my shape, distorted and tall.
Now I am large,
wider than an elephant.
Never been this thin,
garden rakes spring to mind.

Different sizes, strange looks.
All me, yet not really me.
A strange twist of who I am.
Something weird, not ringing true.

'Let us make man in our image,'
the Maker created us to be.
Then came the great Fall,
sin distorts our image,
making it no fun at all.

Genesis chapter 3; Romans 6:23, Romans 3:23

Q Why do you think Adam and Eve ate the fruit?
A

Q How were they tricked?
A

Q What were the consequences of their actions?
A

Q What are the consequences of sin in our lives?
A

Q What has God done about our sin?
A

Any comments on what you've read:

Any questions you'd like to ask:

Unit 4

Who is Jesus?

Dear Jake,

Thanks for your last letter. I don't really think I understand it all, about suffering I mean, but it did help. Next time Dad says God's to blame, I'll tell him he is to blame and not God. What do you think?

There is another reason why I'm writing. Guess what? I have another question. Are you getting fed up with all my questions? Bet you are. Tell me if you are. I'd hate to be a pain.

I do know a little bit about what I believe, and I do read my Bible, well sometimes, bits of it anyway. The problem is trying to explain what I believe to my family 'cos they're always having a go at me, apart from my mum — she never stops to sit down, never mind talk. It's my dad and brother, they're the ones who have a right go at me. They say they're only joking but they don't make me laugh. Anyway, this is what happened the other night.

We have Sky TV at our house, as if we don't watch enough telly. Dad wants it for all the sport. He's a big Man U. fan, and they're on every other day. My brother supports Man U. as well. Well, the other night, Man U. had a big FA Cup match. It was a replay against Barnsley, whoever they are. Dad was sitting with a can of beer in his hand, shouting at the telly. You'd think they could hear him the way he carries on. Mind you, he shouts loud enough, they probably can!

Dad kept going on about how Man U. were going to stuff Barnsley. Said Barnsley hadn't even got a prayer, then looked at me and laughed. Dad stopped laughing when Barnsley scored twice. That's when he said it: 'Jesus!'

He just said it the once, but he said it so loud, and it was the way he said it. It was horrible. I have heard lots of people talk about Jesus and sing about him on camp, but it was different with Dad. He was cursing, swearing I suppose. When he said it I felt my toes curl and something inside snapped. I'm not very good at this self-control bit.

'Dad!' I shouted.

'Did you see that?' Dad was still pointing at the TV.

'Dad!'

'What?'

'Don't say that again.'

'What?'

'You know.' Dad was still watching the match.

'Dad.'

'What?' This time he turned to me.

'Don't say that again.'

'Say what? What are you on about?'

'You know.'

'No, I don't.'

'Jesus.'

'Eh?'

'You took his name in vain or something.'

'Well, he's forgiving.'

Dad laughed when he said this. Thought it was a huge joke. He wasn't laughing at the end of the match though, 'cos Man U. lost 3-2 to Barnsley. Dad was muttering and cursing as he went out of the room.

'Dad.'

'What now?'

I could tell Dad wasn't happy by the tone of his voice, but I still had to say it.

'I told you miracles still happen.'

'Eh?'

'3-2, 3-2, 3-2 . . .'

Dad stormed out of the house and slammed the door behind him.

'What have you done to upset your dad?' Mum said as she came in the room.

'Nothing.'

'It's all because of Jesus,' my brother butted in.

'What about him?' Mum asked.

'Dad mentioned him and Sam got upset. Can't see why. He doesn't even exist, does he? Imagine getting upset about someone who doesn't even exist. That's how daft he is.' My brother pointed at me and started laughing. If my mum hadn't been standing there, I would have said something back. Jesus does exist, doesn't he? Why do people use his name as a swear word? Can you help me, Jake?

Yours, needing further help and reassurance,

Sam

Dear Sam,

Thanks for your letter. It was good to hear from you again and no, I don't mind you writing! I said it before and I will say it again, write as much as you want and ask what you want. I may not be able to give a good answer, but I'll do my best.

In answer to your last two questions, I have enclosed some notes and a quiz I used recently in a local high school. Once a week I help run a Christian club at lunch time. Is there one at your school? Do you go? Sorry, Sam, you were the one asking the questions and I was the one supposed to be answering.

Jesus does exist. The notes should help fill in some details, and also hopefully help with your understanding of who Jesus is.

In answer to your question, 'Why do people use his name as a swear word?' I'm afraid I don't really know. I don't like it either. It's like someone saying 'Oh Jake!' every time they lose their temper. I don't think anyone would like it if their name was used in such a way. I don't think people really consider what they're saying or why. It is sad though and sometimes it angers me too. If only people realised who Jesus is! So here are my notes. Hope you find them helpful.

Yours sincerely,

Jake

PS I don't think it would be a good idea to tell your dad he is to blame for everything wrong in the world. The Bible makes it clear that we are all sinners. We have all done things wrong.
PPS Great win for the Super- Reds! Barnsley I mean. My football team!!

Myth . . . make believe . . . or Messiah?

Who is Jesus Christ? A figment of our overworked imaginations? A mythical figure shrouded in the mists of time? A good person who was cruelly killed? Or God's Son, the Messiah, our Saviour?

Let's look through the pages of history and examine the evidence. Which of the following characters are mythical (i.e. legendary with no strong historical evidence to support them), which are fictional (completely made up, an invention of someone's imagination), and which are historical (they really did exist and there is strong evidence to support this)?

1. Winston Churchill
2. Socrates
3. Alfred the Grumble
4. Scrooge
5. King Arthur
6. Jesus
7. Robin Hood
8. Alexander the Great
9. Charles Dickens
10. Sherlock Holmes

Answers

1 historical, 2 historical, 3 fictional, 4 fictional, 5 mythical, 6 historical, 7 mythical, 8 historical, 9 historical, 10 fictional

How did you score on the test? Ten out of ten? What did you say about Jesus Christ? Whatever you said, thought, or believed, the answer is that Jesus is a historical figure. He is not a legendary person or a fictitious character, but someone who actually lived and breathed on this planet two thousand years ago. No historian would doubt or deny that fact. There are a number of historical documents which relate to Jesus, not just the Bible. People may reject Jesus as the Son of God but they cannot say that he did not exist.

If Jesus is real and not a mythical figure, then who was he? Have you ever seen any of those super-heroes on TV? The ones with the hopeless masks and disguises? Superman who, by popping on a pair of glasses, manages to fool everyone and keep his identity a secret. These characters fly or leap around from place to place saving the world before returning to their desk at work. The super-heroes are so unbelievably amazing. The feats they can perform are absolutely incredible, mind-boggling. Our only problem is that however wonderful they are, they do not exist. Too good to be true.

Jesus Christ is a *real* super-hero. The greatest hero who ever lived, and he did not disguise his identity behind a mask or a costume.

For God so loved the world that he gave his one and only Son, that whoever believes in him shall not perish but have everlasting life.' John 3:16

God sent his Son, Jesus, into this world. That is the true identity of Jesus: he is God's Son.

For God did not send his Son into the world to condemn the world, but to save the world through him. John 3:17

God sent his Son, Jesus, into the world for a special reason, a mission to complete. It was no small task. That is why he sent his Son. It was not something that anyone could do. It was something that only Jesus could do . . .

SAVE THE WORLD!

That sounds like a job for a real super-hero, a true super-hero. Enter upon the stage of life the only one capable of performing such a task: Jesus Christ.

Jesus did not hide his identity as God's Son but revealed it by his life, his words, his actions. In fact, every single thing he said and did points to who he is. If you were on a jury in a courtroom you would have to weigh up all of the evidence before you made your verdict.

Let's look at the evidence for Jesus being God's Son.

The things he did . . .

Exhibit 1
Water turned into wine at a wedding feast (John 2:1-11).

Exhibit 2
A paralytic is lowered down through the roof of a house by his friends. He leaves the building by picking up his mat and walking (Luke 5:17-26).

Exhibit 3
Jesus stops a funeral procession in its tracks by asking the dead man to get up (Luke 7:11-17).

Exhibit 4
The disciples think they are going to drown in a furious squall out on a lake until Jesus orders the storm to stop (Luke 8:22-25).

Exhibit 5
A large crowd of over 5,000 eat their fill as Jesus feeds them in a miraculous fashion (Matthew 14:13-21).

Jesus, the Creator of life, demonstrated his power over the whole natural order of creation: from the changing of water to wine, the multiplication of bread and fish, the calming of the waves on the lake, the healing of a man's body and the resurrection from the dead. Who else, but the Creator of the entire universe, could perform such deeds?

The things he said . . .

Exhibit 6
Jesus was found in the temple courts speaking to all the teachers. He was only 12 years old and he was amazing people by what he said. When asked by his parents what he was doing there he replied, 'Didn't you know I had to be in my Father's house?' (Luke 2:41-52)

Exhibit 7
Jesus spoke in the synagogue in his home town of Nazareth and stirred people up by what he said he had come to do (Luke 4:14-30).

Exhibit 8
Jesus says he has the power to forgive sins (Luke 5:17-26).

Exhibit 9
Jesus says anyone who hears his words and puts them into practice is a wise man (Luke 6:46-49).

Exhibit 10
Jesus teaches people how to pray (Luke 11:1-13).

Only God's Son could say and teach all of these things.

Jesus could not have been just a good teacher. He was, and still is, God's one and only Son.

This is evidence that demands a verdict. What is your verdict?

Read all of the stories listed in exhibits one to ten.

Q Why do you think Jesus came to earth?
A

Q How did Jesus save us?
A

Q What do the miracles teach us about Jesus?
A

Q What did you find most striking about what Jesus said?
A

Q Sum up the life of Jesus in one sentence:
A

Any comments on what you've read:

Any questions you'd like to ask:

Unit 5

Did Jesus really rise from the dead?

Dear Jake,

Barnsley! Barnsley! You support Barnsley? I can't believe it. Who on earth supports Barnsley? Nobody at my school. I told my mates that I knew a Barnsley fan and they laughed their socks off. Barnsley! Oh well, nobody's perfect, are they?

Sorry, Jake, I don't mean to go on, but Barnsley! Sorry. That isn't the reason I've written, honest. Your last letter was really helpful. All that stuff about Jesus being a historical figure and all those notes showing he is God's Son. That really helped me. Problem is, you've probably guessed already, my family. I do love them, honest. But sometimes they drive me up the wall, round the bend, down the street, across the road, and all over town. In short, they drive me nuts. I tried to pray the other night and to ask God to give me peace and patience but I couldn't even get my words out. My dad had the TV on full blast, my brother had his stereo on at top volume and Mum decided to do some hoovering. At 10.30 at night!! She said she saw a crumb behind Dad's chair and couldn't rest until she got it. No peace in our house! Anyway, Jake, that's not why I'm writing — it's what my dad said that's bothering me. I just wish I had the answers for him but I haven't. Everything blew up last weekend, Easter Sunday. I was planning to go to church because it was Easter Day, my dad had other plans. I was just putting my coat on, about to leave the house when Dad collared me.

'Where do you think you are going?' It was more an accusation than a question.

'Church,' I replied.

'Church?'

'Yeah, Church.'

'Church?'

'Are you a parrot, Dad?'

'A parrot?'

'Yeah — you keep repeating everything I say.'

'Watch your lip, young man.'

I know I shouldn't have said those things but it was the way Dad said 'church' that got to me. It was if I had some vile disease. Then Dad got really mad.

'Why bother going to church?' he said.

'It's Easter, Dad. You know – Jesus rising from the dead and all that.'

'Well, no, I don't know Jesus and I don't know anybody who can come back to life again. It's impossible. If you believe that, you'll believe anything. You're like a sponge, soaking up anything you come across.'

'You're wrong, Dad, I don't just believe in anything.'

'You believe that Jesus came back to life?'

'Yeah.'

'Sponge!'

'Dad!'

'Come on, I'd planned for us to go to the coast for the day. You don't want to go to church – it's much more fun at the beach.'

There was a long pause and then I said, 'Jesus came to give us life in all its fullness.'

'What?'

It was something I remembered one of the leaders saying at camp. I just blurted it out. I hadn't a clue what to say next.

'How can Jesus give you anything when he's dead? Now get in the car – we're going to the coast.'

I was going to shout at him, but for some reason, I didn't. I sat and sulked in the car all the way to the beach though. Told my dad I didn't enjoy the day at all, although seeing my brother drenched through by a big wave was a good laugh!

Jake, I know Jesus isn't dead, but how can I convince my dad? What does it really mean to have life in all its fullness?

Yours puzzledly,

Sam

Dear Sam,

   Thanks for your letter. It's good to hear from you although I am sad to hear of your arguments with your family. Not that it will make you feel any better but I had similar rows with my family when I was a teenager many years ago!

   How can Jesus give us 'fullness of life' and what proof is there that he really did rise from the dead? Two excellent questions. I would like to share with you a sketch I did in some schools recently and some notes on what you were asking. Once again I hope that these are adequate and helpful.

   Yours sincerely,

   Jake

   PS What's wrong with Barnsley?

   PPS Were you going to church because it was Easter Sunday or do you go every week anyway?

Food for all

Scene

Two people are standing with their backs to the audience. One, a man (M), is looking into a shop. The other, a shopkeeper (SK), is inside. The man outside is very hungry, starving. He walks along the shopfront, standing on tip-toe to look on the shelves, crouching down low to look at what is on offer. The shopkeeper, in the back of the shop, is putting items on his shelves. (It is very important to use your body to create a strong visual picture, as standing with your back to the audience is not usual for drama! It should, however, create a unique picture and be a fresh start to the sketch.)

After lots of looking through the window the man turns round, rubs his stomach and licks his lips. He moves towards the door, opens it and enters the shop.

SK   Good morning.

M   Hello!

The shopkeeper is very friendly but the shopper is very nervous

SK   Anything I can help you with?

M   Just looking.

SK   Feel free.

The shopkeeper smiles and turns away to carry on with stacking the shelves. The shopper starts to wander round the shop, looking at all the items. Sometimes he stops to have a close inspection. He eventually stops when he sees something he really wants. As he stands staring his mouth begins to water

M   Excuse me, please.

SK   Yes, Sir, how can I help?

M   I was looking for a price.

SK   A price?

M   Yes, I don't seem to be able to find one anywhere. Not here *(Man points to what he is looking at)*. Nor on any other item in the shop *(He sweeps his arm round to indicate what he means)*. No prices anywhere.

The shopkeeper comes from behind the counter, he has a huge grin on his face

SK   Is the price important, Sir?

M   Very. *(The shopper is starting to become agitated, he is very hungry)* How much?

SK   To you, Sir?

M   Yes, of course to me. You don't see anyone else in the shop do you? *(The man turns round)* Oh look, there's a herd of elephants coming through the door. Be careful. BE CAREFUL! Don't all crowd, there's room for everyone, enough food to feed . . . an elephant actually!

SK   Really, Sir?

M   Look, I'm sorry. I shouldn't have said all of that. It's just that . . . *(He stops and looks at the shopkeeper)* . . . I haven't eaten for days. I managed to find a few pence on the streets and . . . your food looks so good . . . but I don't think I can afford any of it.

SK   Really, Sir?

M   Really.

SK   What do you want, Sir?

M   A free ticket to EuroDisney or maybe a free year's subscription to the *Reader's Digest*. What do you think I want? I want to eat of course! *(He glares at the shopkeeper, then holds his head in shame)* I'm sorry. It's just that when you've not eaten . . .

SK   I understand, Sir.

M   You do?

SK   Whatever you want to eat is yours. It's all free!

M   Free?

SK   Free.

M   FREE!?

SK   All for free.

The man is delighted and picks up some food

M   Wait a minute, this isn't a wind-up ,is it?

Shopkeeper shakes his head

M   How come your food's free?

SK   Well, it's not really free.

M   I knew it! I knew there was a catch. *(He slams his food back down)*

SK   No catch, Sir, the food is free to you.

M   Eh?

SK   I paid for it.

M   What? Are you trying to tell me that you paid for all this wonderful food, only to give it away?

SK   To all those who are hungry and needy … yes!

M   Then why doesn't everyone come?

SK   That's a very good question, Sir.

     Freeze

Some verses that show the meaning of the sketch in the words of the Bible …

Isaiah 55:1-3a
Come, all you who are thirsty, come to the waters; and you who have no money, come buy and eat! Come, buy wine and milk, without money and without cost. Why spend money on what is not bread, and your labour on what does not satisfy? Listen, listen to me, and eat what is good, and your soul will delight in the richest of fare. Give ear and come to me; hear me that your soul may live.

John 6:33-35
For the bread of God is he who comes down from heaven and gives life to the world. 'Sir,' they said, 'from now on give us this bread.' Then Jesus declared, 'I am the bread of life. He who comes to me will never go hungry, and he who believes in me will never be thirsty.'

We know that we need food so that we can physically live, but what about our spiritual life?

Jesus answers this question by declaring that he is the bread of life. Not a wholemeal loaf, but the one who can satisfy our deepest needs. Jesus came into this world to show us how to live a complete life and to also offer that life to anyone who chooses. He offers us his very life.

Jesus can do that because he rose from the dead. He is alive for evermore.

Jesus can do that because he is God.

Jesus can do that because the third person of the trinity, the Holy Spirit, can live within us.

Deep theology here, but dynamite living!

Raving mad, really bad or resurrection reality?

Your best friend has just died. You are devastated. Life isn't the same anymore. Not only did he die, but people killed him. He was murdered. The shock of what has happened has sickened you to the core. Could life get any worse? Yes. The same people who killed your friend may come after you next! What a horrible world you are existing in. One moment all your hopes and dreams are being fulfilled in front of your eyes, the next you are walking around in a living nightmare. What's going to happen now?

You run out into the town square. You shout at the top of your voice. Your friend is alive again! Everyone saw him die – what's going on? What are the possible explanations for your behaviour? Have you lost your marbles? Are you merely a deceiver, or are you telling the truth?

The choices are many. But there is only one answer. Only one of the above can be the truth. Which one is it?

As we look at and examine the lives of the disciples we see that they point us to only one conclusion.

On the night Jesus was arrested they fled. They were scared men. Jesus died. What could have brought such a transformation in terrified hearts? Perhaps one of the disciples could have made up a fantastical story of Jesus being alive again. Perhaps the pressure had played on his grey cells and he was no longer in control of his mental faculties. What about the rest of the disciples? If they had all cracked up under the strain would they all have the same story to tell? Would they have the capacity to preach in public? The mathematical odds of all the disciples going ga-ga are beyond calculation. It is an absurdity to believe such an idea.

So why did they say they had seen Jesus alive again?

Deceivers. Not demented but deceitful. They wanted to save face so they told bare-faced lies. Is that the truth? What about when they were arrested, imprisoned, beaten and killed? If they knew Jesus was really dead would they all have allowed themselves to go through such suffering? It is absurd to think so.

What then is the truth? Which possible explanation remains standing?

The resurrection really happened. Jesus was alive again. Jesus is alive today. That is why the lives of the disciples were changed, that's why Christianity is alive 2000 years on.

Jesus came to give us life in all its fullness. That life is Jesus himself. The Son of God, who was crucified but rose again, who once was dead but has now defeated death; Jesus Christ who can live within us by the power of the Holy Spirit. Jesus, the risen Lord.

Read John 10:7-10, and the whole of John 20

Q In John 10, what promise does Jesus make?
A

Q Are there any other ways offered to find fulfilment in life?
A

Q In John 20, what were the initial reactions of the disciples when Jesus wasn't in the tomb?
A

Q How did that change?
A

Q What evidence is there for the resurrection?
A

Any comments on what you've read:

Any questions you'd like to ask:

Unit 6

Who is the Holy Spirit?

Dear Jake,

Hi! It's me again, Sam. Thanks for your last letter. I enjoyed reading your sketch. Wish the shopkeepers where I live gave everything away for nothing! Perhaps I'll ask them next time. What do you think?

Guess what? You'll never guess. You can try if you want, but you'll not guess it. I've been to church! Last Sunday. Not only have I been but my mum came with me! It all came as a result of going to the seaside with my family. Remember, I didn't want to go because it was Easter Sunday. I wanted to go to church but Dad said we were all going to the coast. The day after our trip, Bank Holiday Monday, there was a knock on my bedroom door. It was very early, about 10 o'clock. I was still half asleep and could hardly open my eyes, let alone speak.

'Go away,' I said.

The knock came again.

'Go away,' I shouted.

The knock was even louder.

'What d'ya want?' I asked.

Mum was in my room like a shot. 'Do you want to go to church, love?' she said.

'Not now, Mum.'

'No, not now, love. Next week, next Sunday.'

My head shot up like a catapult from the pillow. 'Church?'

'Yes.'

'Next Sunday?'

'Yes.'

'With you?'

'Yes, love, with me,' she said as she smiled.

I gave my mum my best cheesy smile, then flopped back on to the bed exhausted. The following Sunday we nearly didn't make it to church. We nearly didn't make it out of the house.

'Come on, Mum, hurry up!'

'I'll be down in a minute.'

That was code for 'I'll be there in 10 minutes after I've applied 5 coats of make-up!'

'Mum! We'll be late.'

I heard doors slamming upstairs then a thud-thud-thud as Mum came racing down the stairs.

'Great. We can go now.'

I turned towards the door.

'You're not ready!' Mum's voice was very high-pitched with a hint of hysteria.

'I am.'

'But you're wearing jeans!!'

I was tempted to give my mum a big round of applause for her sharp observational skills but thought that might not be the best thing to do. So I simply stated my case. 'They're clean.'

'Church, Samuel!'

She never calls me Samuel.

'It's Sunday and we're going to church. When I was a little girl I always wore my best clothes when I went to church.'

I never knew Mum went to church when she was a girl.

'Get changed or we're not going!'

I looked at my mum and gave her my best 'I'm not very pleased about all this' face . . .

'Now!' she said.

Coming out of church a few hours later I felt shell-shocked. Church was nothing like camp. The speakers on camp never wore frocks! The preacher's voice reminded me of a lullaby — it kept sending me to sleep. When we went up for Communion I nearly choked on the wine. I thought it was going to be Ribena! No one clapped when we were singing, not that there was a tune to clap along to. 'What on earth would Mum think?' I wondered.

'Lovely service.'

'What?'

'Lovely service, wasn't it, love? Lovely man, that vicar.'

I could hardly believe my ears. 'Lovely' was not the word I would have chosen.

'It's always made me think . . .' (Mum was still going on about the service.)

'. . . When the vicar says, "In the name of the Father, the Son, and the Holy Spirit", I can understand God as Father and Jesus his Son, but I've never understood anything about the Holy Spirit. Do you know?'

Mum suddenly stopped walking and looked straight at me as if I was a walking encyclopaedia of theology.

'The Holy Spirit is . . . is . . . is . . . is the . . . Holy . . . Spirit!' I said triumphantly.

'Oh,' said Mum.

She didn't sound too impressed.

When we got home I started thinking. Who is the Holy Spirit? What does he really do? I wish I really did know. I wish I could tell Mum, too.

Jake, can you help please?

Sam

Dear Sam,

Thanks for your last letter. It was good to hear from you again. You were quite right too. I didn't guess that you had been to church with your mum. I am really pleased that you have been even if it wasn't quite what you had expected! I hope that you will not be too put off and try again, especially if your mum is keen to go – that's great news.

The Holy Spirit. THE Holy Spirit. The HOLY Spirit. The Holy SPIRIT. What a big subject. Yet it is important to realise right at the beginning that the Holy Spirit isn't a subject, or a topic, or a concept, but a person, a part of the God-head, the trinity. God in three persons, Father, Son and Holy Spirit. This can be very confusing to think of God in three parts. Yet the world we live in gives us pictures and reminders that this is distinctly possible. H_2O can appear in various shapes and sizes: ice, steam and water. They are all H_2O and they are all very different. H_2O can take the form of a liquid, gas or solid. It sounds incredible but we know it is not impossible, we know it is true. When we think of God it is important to see God as three persons. God, the Father; God, the Son; and God, the Holy Spirit. Thinking about God as Spirit can be very confusing.

The church today has all kinds of teaching regarding the Holy Spirit. Some of it can be a little conflicting or a little confusing. I am not the world's expert on the Holy Spirit! What I want to try to express above everything else is that the Holy Spirit is a person. He is a part of the trinity and he plays a powerful and crucial role in our lives.

I have enclosed three articles on the Holy Spirit: an A to Z, a general guide to understanding who he is, then a look at his gifts and fruits. I hope these are helpful to you (and to your mum!).

Yours sincerely, Jake

PS I didn't mention football once! PPS Oops, I just did!!!

An A-Z of the Holy Spirit

Alpha   The Holy Spirit was right there in the beginning with God and Jesus. He was involved in the creation of the world (Genesis 1:2).

Bravery   The disciples who had fled when Jesus was arrested ran out into the market square to tell everyone Jesus was alive when they had been filled with the Holy Spirit (Acts 2).

Counsellor   The Holy Spirit promised to his disciples by Jesus (John 14:16).

Deposit   The Holy Spirit is with us now, guaranteeing what is to come (2 Corinthians 5:5).

Eternal   The promise of eternal life with God (2 Corinthians 5:5).

Filled   The disciples were filled with the Holy Spirit (Acts 2).

Gifts   The Holy Spirit gives spiritual gifts (1 Corinthians 14).

Holy   The Holy Spirit is HOLY!

Indwelling   He lives within us (John 14:17).

Jesus   The Son of God was filled with the Spirit of God (John 1:32).

Kingdom   God's Kingdom isn't set out with boundaries but is in the hearts of his people.

Life   The Holy Spirit gives spiritual life to us (Ephesians 2:1-10 and Romans 8:11).

Mirror   We were made in God's image. The Holy Spirit helps us to be like God (Genesis 1:27).

Never   Never will God leave us or forsake us; he has given his Holy Spirit to us (Hebrews 13:5).

Omnipresent   God is everywhere (Psalm 139).

Person   Never forget that the Holy Spirit is a person, not an 'it'.

Quiet	God's Spirit can speak to us in the stillness and quiet of our own hearts.
Revival	Only God's Spirit can bring about mass revival, miracles and healings.
Salvation	The Holy Spirit is a seal of our salvation (Ephesians 1:13-14).
Trust	We walk by faith and not by sight. God's Spirit can guide and lead us.
Understanding	The Holy Spirit helps to make scripture understandable (Psalm 119:18).
Victory	Power over sin and death.
Wholeness.	The Holy Spirit helps make us the people God created us to be (Romans 12:2).
eXonerated	We are no longer under condemnation, but set free from sin (Romans 8:1).
You	The Holy Spirit comes to live in your life.
Zion	A new home awaits all of God's children.

Christmas in God's house

At last! No more anxious clock-watching. No more creeping around in the dark. No more peeking under the tree. The waiting was over. Today was the day. Christmas.

Presents strewn around the tree as you fly towards it breaking the land-speed record. The gift tags give you the vital information – which ones are yours.

You look frantically through the pile of pressies until at last your eyes alight on the ones marked for you.

Breathless with anticipation you tear through the paper. You find the present buried deep inside the wrapping. You hold up aloft your new treasured possession.

A pair of grey and brown chequered socks!

You swiftly check through the paper, eyes scanning for the gift tag. You find it. You look closely at the name. Your name. Unmistakably written in bold letters. The socks belong to you!

Oh well, one mistake, one bad present isn't too disastrous. Your search for presents resumes with a speed that Speedy Gonzales would be impressed with.

Minutes later you sit on the carpeted floor surrounded by your Christmas presents: a year's subscription to *The Businessman's Guide to Maggot Farming*; a Black and Decker lawnmower with deluxe super-shaped, super-sharp blades and a set of silk, name-emblazoned handkerchiefs.

Your presents. You stare in disbelief. Is this a nightmare or what?

The alarm rings.

Your head jumps off the pillow. You look at the time. It's Christmas morning. You realise you've been dreaming. What a nightmare. Now it's time to open the real presents!

No decent parent would give their child presents they didn't want. God is a good, perfect Father. Through the Holy Spirit God gives gifts to his children. The gifts are different, not always the same for each child but always good and always ideally suited. There is no need to take back and exchange God's gifts. They are perfect. The only shame is when we don't use the gifts God has given us. How many people would leave their presents under the tree? Why not unwrap the gifts God has given you? Discover them, then use them. If you enjoy Christmas, then you'll love God's presents and you don't have to wait until Christmas for them!

How does your garden grow?

When I was 11 I moved house. Not just me, but my whole family! The house we moved to had a nice back garden. Not too big, but big enough to play cricket in and because it was summer that was exactly what my brother and I spent our time doing.

In our garden we had a big apple tree. It was a lovely tree, standing tall and proud, with its branches protruding in all directions declaring to the whole wide world 'Look at my apples!' The problem was our apple tree did attract attention. If not the whole world, certainly our neighbourhood.

One day I was coming home from school and heard noises coming from our garden. I peeked a look and saw a group of boys standing around our apple tree. They were looking up. Sitting on the branches was a boy busy picking off all our apples. I raced down to the tree and joined the gang.

'Hey!' I whispered in a conspiratorial tone.

'What do you want?' said the boy up the tree.

'How about some apples?'

'OK,' said the lad. He picked off some more apples and scrambled down the tree.

'I think I'll have all of them.' The boy looked at me in disbelief. 'It is my tree!' I said.

Within seconds the garden was empty apart from me, that is, and a lot of apples!

Now here's the tough question. I hope you've been reading carefully. Here goes . . .

What fruit was growing on the tree?

Next tough question . . .

What kind of tree was it?

If you answered 'apple' you answered correctly. Apple trees grow apples. They do not grow bananas, oranges, pears, lamb chops, peanut butter, umbrellas or lamp stands! Apple trees grow apples. That is what they were created to do and will only produce the fruit specific to an apple tree.

Excuse me, but I thought we were talking about the Holy Spirit? Yes, we are. Let's look at Galatians 5:22 . . .

The fruit of the Spirit is love, joy, peace, patience, kindness, goodness, faithfulness, gentleness and self-control.

What kind of characteristics should we be producing as Christians? All of the above! When the Holy Spirit lives within us then that is the fruit he will help us to bear. Remember it's the fruit of his Spirit – not our own goodness, but God's goodness.

Read Galatians 5:16-26

Q Who is the Holy Spirit?
A

Q How does he produce fruit in our lives?
A

Q What hinders the work of the Holy Spirit?
A

Q How can we keep in step with the Spirit?
A

Q Give three words which describe the Holy Spirit:
1.
2.
3.

Any comments on what you've read:

Any questions you'd like to ask:

Unit 7

Why go to church?

Dear Jake,

Thanks for writing back to me again. Are you sure you're not fed up by now? Anyway, thanks for all those notes on the Holy Spirit. I did learn a lot although I'm not sure if I could take it all in; there was a lot of information, not that I'm complaining! I make sure that I keep all the notes that you send me somewhere safe; that way I can look at them when I need to. Bet you're impressed with me now, not that I'm trying to show off, honest!

Why I am writing this time is to ask you about church. Remember, Mum and I went a few weeks ago. Can you also remember that Mum wasn't very happy with me going to church dressed in my jeans? I don't know if I told you in my letter but I did get changed. I wore a suit. Please don't faint or laugh, it's not funny. I wore a suit. Me, Sam, walking down the high street in a brand-new three-piece job. It's only the second time I've worn it. The first time was at cousin Freda's wedding, that's the reason why I got the suit. Mum and Dad insisted. I told them I'd got a tie, my school one, but they just laughed. I wasn't joking, so I don't know why they found it so funny. Anyway, that's why I came to be wearing a suit a couple of weeks ago. I got changed the second I got back home and never thought about the suit after that, not until Monday morning first lesson, science with Mr Einstein (that's not his real name). I was sitting in my usual seat, somewhere near the back of the class, listening to old Einstein explaining some scientific law or other when a pellet struck my ear lobe. Thankfully it was only a paper pellet. It bounced straight of my ear and landed on the floor. I looked round and saw a big toothy grin from one of my so-called class-mates. I decided to ignore him.

'Oi!'

I still was going to ignore him.

'Oi!'

It was getting louder.

'Oi!'

This time Einstein stopped talking. Only for a split second then he carried on.

'Oi!'

This time I turned around.

'Pick it up.'

Another big toothy grin was flashed in my direction. Realising I wasn't going to be left in peace until I picked up the piece of paper, I leaned over, scooped it up and placed it on my desk.

When Einstein turned his back I quickly unfolded the paper. I then quickly folded it again. I then even quicker than quick unfolded it. My heart was racing and I could feel my ribcage shaking. I looked down at the piece of paper. I stared in horror at the drawing scrawled all over it, a horrible picture of me, standing next to my mum with my suit on! There were two arrows pointing to me. One said, 'Who's a lovely mummy's boy,' the other said, 'What a lovely, lovely suit, how cool, NOT!!'

It felt as if my face had been set on fire. My cheeks must have turned bright red. If they were any hotter I would set the class on fire. I had been seen in my suit with my mum! What could I say? What were my class-mates going to say?

Somehow, Jake, I avoided them for the rest of the day. Probably because I hid in the toilets all lunch break. On my way out of the school gates I could sense freedom, escape, all until . . .

'Oi, Sammy, Sammy suit boy. Sammy, mummy's boy, what ya doing?'

I carried on walking as if I hadn't heard.

'Why wear a suit, Sammy? You looked like you were going to church.'

I kept on walking.

'Or a funeral.'

'Same thing.'

Someone else shouted then there was lots of laughing and I started running.

Jake, what if people saw me going to church. They'll think I'm really sad and boring. Why should I go to church? I found it really boring. Mum wants to go again; she says it's a lovely building, lovely windows. It's not like camp! What is church? What's it all about? Please help because I'm really struggling on this one.

Yours despairingly,

Sam

Dear Sam,

Thanks for your letter. Oh, boy, what a situation! I do sympathise with you Sam. Being picked on and laughed at for any reason is horrible. It's wrong and it shouldn't happen, but sadly it does. Not that there's anything to laugh at. There is nothing wrong or funny about going to church or wearing smart clothes. I wear a suit sometimes when I go to church. Nothing wrong in that. A lot of people prefer to wear their best clothes when they go to church. I do hope and trust that your friends won't carry on their mickey-taking. I am sure it will soon blow over although I know that was no consolation at the time. I do remember what it's like being at school . . . just!

To try to answer your questions Sam, I have enclosed a sketch and some notes. The church is very important and . . . well, I'll let you read the notes! Please let me know how you get on at school and at church.

Yours hopefully helpfully,

Jake

People, places and presence

The Church is a name given to God's people. In the Old Testament God's people were the nation of Israel, in the New Testament we see a change. We see believers from different countries and different cultures. Race is no longer an issue, real faith is.

God's people need to meet together. They usually require a place to do this. Although if the weather is nice you could meet outside, in the park, on the beach or on a street corner. Mostly we choose to meet in a building. It is practical. Some people find that for them the building is important; a cross can remind them of their Saviour who died for their sins. The beautiful architecture can create a sense of awe and wonder – a helpful reminder of the awesome and wonderful God we worship. For some people the building is not important. They would equally be happy worshipping in a school hall or a sports centre or a house or a big tent. What is vitally important for all Christians is that they meet with God.

> *Where two or three are gathered in my name, I am with them.*
> Matthew 19:20

Jesus made a promise to be with his followers, present in their midst. God is with us individually through his Holy Spirit but there is something very special about Christians meeting together.

Church is all about God's people meeting together and meeting with God. We worship him, we learn about him, and we love one another as we come closer to God.

Church will never be perfect because we are not perfect but if God is present, it is the place to be – a priority for all of God's people.

Watching the grass grow!

Two people are standing side by side.

Bill   Hey, Burt, it brings back memories.

Burt   Aye, Bill.

Bill   What memories, hey, Burt?

Burt   What memories, Bill?

Bill   What memories? Can't you remember?

Burt   Remember?

Bill   Stood here as a lad *(He takes a deep breath and lets out a huge sigh)*. Memories.

Burt   Memories?

Bill   Look at that stand, Burt.

Burt   Beautiful.

Bill   Work of modern art.

Burt   Wonderful.

Bill   I never sat there.

Burt   No, me neither.

Bill   Fantastic stand.

Burt   Fabulous.

Bill   Look at them lights.

Burt   Massive.

Bill   You could light up the whole town with those lights.

Burt   You could light up my garden shed with those lights.

        Bill stares at Burt

Burt   It's very dark in my garden shed.

Bill   Look at that grass, Burt.

Burt   Green, isn't it?

Bill   Cut to perfection; so smooth you could play snooker on it.

Burt   I think they play football on it, Bill.

Bill   Of course they do, it was just a metaphor.

Burt   Meant for who?

Bill   Forget it.

Burt   I never got it!

Bill   Look around you, Burt.

    Burt has a look

Burt   There's no one there, Bill.

Bill   I know that, Burt.

Burt   Oh. So what are we looking around for? There's only us here.

Bill   We're looking at the ground, the stadium: a cathedral.

Burt   There's no stained glass.

Bill   Hey?

Burt   Cathedrals. I think they have stained glass windows with pictures on.

Bill   It was another metaphor.

Burt   Meant for . . .

Bill   Forget it!

Burt   Forgotten.

Bill   I love this ground. The seats, the stands, the floodlights, the grass, the . . .

Burt   Coming on Saturday?

Bill   What?

Burt   To see the Reds play.

Bill   Oh no. I don't come to the games.

Burt   Oh. I just thought . . .

Bill   Yeah?

Burt   Forget it.

Bill   Forgotten.

Burt   It is a nice ground.

    Bill looks around, takes a big breath, then sighs

Bill   I could live here, it would be paradise.

Burt   Don't you like living on our street?

Bill   It was just a meta . . .

        They look at each other

Both   Forget it!

As great as football stadiums may be, that is not why we go there. We do not go to admire the decor or the grass or the lights, or the stands – we go to watch football and support our team. Grounds vary, some are better than others but they are irrelevant when it comes to our reason for being in them. When people think of Church they often think of a building, but Church isn't bricks and mortar – it's people. Just as going to a football ground is about going to watch the football and not the ground, so 'going to church' is about what goes on inside the building and not the building itself!

What am I?
I am young,
I am old.
I am black,
I am white.
I am a bride.
I am living stones.
I am the apple of his eye.
I am . . .

. . . the Church

Read Acts 2:42-47

Q Why do you think Church is important?

A

Q From reading the verses in Acts, why do you think the first Christians thought it was important to meet together?

A

Q What does the poem 'What am I?' show about the way God sees the Church?

A

Q Why is there no perfect Church?

A

Q What advice would you give Sam about how to deal with the mickey-taking at school?

A

Any comments on what you've read:

Any questions you'd like to ask:

Unit 8

What is a good Church?

Dear Jake,

Thanks for your last letter. You were right! The next day I went to school dreading it. In my sleep I kept having nightmares of walking into assembly and seeing a massive drawing of me in my suit, and the moment I set foot in the hall all eyes were on me . . . everyone laughing. People coming right up into my face and howling like hyenas. It was horrible. I kept waking up only to doze off again and have another vivid dream of me being chased around the corridors with people chanting, 'Mummy's boy, Mummy's boy, bet you still play with Lego and toys.'

You can imagine how I felt when I walked through the school gates. A nervous wreck. I kept my head down and marched quickly into school. In assembly there was no giant picture of me. In the corridor, no one was chasing me or chanting my name. In the classroom no one made fun of me! It was as if they had all forgotten. All my mates were talking about was the England match the night before. I was history. It had all blown over like you said it would. I was so happy I felt like standing on my desk and shouting 'Hallelujah'. (I have seen gospel singers on TV do that. Not stand on desks! Shout 'Hallelujah' I mean.) Only I thought I'd better not because if I did I would have the mickey taken out of me for the rest of the year for sure.

Jake, sorry to waffle but I was so relieved I wanted to tell you about it.

Church. Church. Jake, I read your letter and tried to understand why Church is so important. I don't know if I understood that poem. Sorry, I don't mean to be rude but I don't see myself as a lily and certainly not a bride! I showed the poem to my mum and she said, 'Oh that's lovely,' then carried on dusting. Anyway Jake, even if I didn't quite understand it all, I did get the picture that Church is important. God's people getting together and all that. So

I went again the following week with Mum. This time Dad took us in the car. It was raining. I was glad because it meant Dad dropped us off and said he would be back in one hour, if it was still raining.

Inside the church the minister, the one with the frock, nearly squeezed all the blood out of my hand. I was dying to shout out, scream actually, but I just bit my lip and tried to smile at him. Not easy smiling when you've just bit into your gum and you can feel it starting to bleed. Mum was happy, smiling at everyone as if she knew them and saying things like: 'Oh, it does remind me of being a little girl again.'

I thought she was going to start skipping down the aisle! I've never seen Mum so happy. I don't really know why either. All I could see was a lot of people in suits and big hats with flowers and gardens growing in them! I looked around for anyone my age. Not being very good at maths I wondered how long it would take me to calculate it all. Not very long.

Two.

Two young people. Two teenagers and one of them was me! Still, I tried to remember how important it was to be there so I thought I would listen really carefully to what the bloke had to say.

After a few minutes I found my mind wandering, and I realised that I hadn't got a clue what the vicar was on about. Then my eyelids got all heavy, and before I knew it, I'd nodded off! To my delight I started dreaming that I was the best striker in the best footie team in the country. It was the last few minutes of the cup final, and it was one all . . . I took possession . . . weaved in and out right down the field . . . and there it was . . .the goal mouth was before me, open wide, ready for me to net the winning goal. A cup final medal was within my grasp.

'Samuel, Samuel, SAM!'

Mum's dulcet tones shot like cannon balls through my ear canal and inside my head. I catapulted so far forward I nearly rammed my head into the pew in front of me. The only thing that stopped me was the woman sitting on the pew in front of me. I thrust my arms out and managed to brake by knocking the woman's head and hat. Her geraniums went flying in the air. She let out the loudest shriek I have ever heard. I don't know what happened next because Mum had dragged me out of church. She made me stand outside, in the pouring rain, whilst she went back inside to apologise.

When she came out she looked all red and flustered. She grabbed hold of my hand and marched me up the High Street.

'We're not going to church again,' she announced.

I said nothing.

'I can never show my face again.'

She looked at me, accusingly. How could I tell her that it was all the minister's fault and hers! If the minister hadn't been so boring I wouldn't have fallen asleep and if Mum hadn't shouted in my ear I wouldn't have shot forward.

I decided to say nothing.

So, Jake, that looks like the end of my church-going. Mum doesn't want to go back and if I go on my own, who is going to wake me up at the end? Perhaps I'll spend the rest of my life in church. It felt like that on Sunday morning. So what do I do, Jake? If Church is so important, how come it's so boring? And if all I do is go to sleep, what point is there? Hope you've got some good answers, Jake.

Yours, needing lots more help and advice,

Sam

Dear Sam,

You do live a very interesting life! You say that Church is boring but it doesn't sound dull when you're around.

'Watch out missus! Keep your hat on!'

Only joking, Sam. I hope you don't mind. It did sound quite comical though, you've got to admit!!

I do sympathise with your struggles. Sadly, for many people (not just young people), Church is boring. And I have to say that I have come across many teenagers who find going to church less interesting than watching paint dry. This is sad because one thing that Church should never be is boring. What I wrote to you in my last letter is true. Church is a very special place. Maybe it would help if I gave a little list of things to look for in a good Church. Not that I'm saying that the one you are going to is a bad one, but again sadly there are so many Churches around and not all of them believe in the Bible or even in Jesus, or the Holy Spirit or God!

Along with my list I have also enclosed a short story about football which I thought you might like.

Please let me know how you get on.

Yours advisingly,

Jake

Ten top tips for choosing a Church

1. A Church that believes in God the Father, God the Son, and God the Holy Spirit.

2. A Church that believes that the Bible is the inspired word of God.

3. A Church that regularly meets together to worship, pray, and study the Word of God.

4. A Church that is caring for its members.

5. A Church that believes in every member been vital and playing an active role.

6. A Church that believes in telling others about Jesus.

7. A Church that is involved in mission.

8. A Church that cares for the poor.

9. A Church that is warm and welcoming to new people.

10. A Church that seeks to put God first in everything.

The building, the denomination or type of service may vary but the above are essential for any Church. Remember, no Church will be perfect but if they are genuinely trying to put their faith into practice they will be a wonderful group to be with.

The team

Nervousness is a very contagious disease. Once you have it there is no set cure. No tablets, no medicines can take it away. Once the nervous system has been breached and attacked, there is a struggle, a fight, a battle within. Nerves have wrecked people's careers.

Looking round the dressing room on that bright afternoon in May, it was easy to see why. Grown men stood with their knees knocking, legs trembling like jellies on a plate. People sat biting their nails, chewing hard right down onto their cuticles. To one another, they presented faces masked with bravado. Behind their disguise was a sea of worry . . .

'What if I don't perform?' 'What if I miss an open goal?' 'What if I score an own goal?' 'What if we lose?'

Gerry Ryan, team captain, folk hero, inspirational, international player spoke up. 'All ready, lads?'

'Yeah! You bet Gerry!' 'Let's show them who's best!' 'Mine's a hat trick!'

'All right then lads, let's go.'

Gerry spun round and sped down the tunnel onto the smooth green surface. The sharp sunlight caught his eyes, making him blink. 'Come on lads, let's do this for the fans.'

Gerry stopped. Normally there would be grunts, shouts, voices chattering behind him. Today there was nothing. Not one single player had made the short journey from the changing rooms onto the pitch. Gerry stood. He waited. Still no one. He glanced around him. The other team were warming up on their half of the pitch. The referee was looking at his watch. Still no one came. Gerry shouted across to the referee. 'Back in a minute ref, won't be long . . .' Then he quickly disappeared inside the tunnel.

'Nice wind-up lads, got me that time. Now come on, let's get cracking.' Gerry turned, began to leave the room, then stopped. No one had moved. 'Lad's? What's going on?'

Sad, sorrowful faces stared up at Gerry. 'Not today, Ges.'

'What do you mean, not today?' asked Gerry.

The big Russian goal-keeper, six foot six in his football socks, held up his little finger. 'It really is hurting, Ges. Sorry.'

Gerry looked round at the rest of his players.

'I've got a bit of a headache coming on, Ges.'

'Last time I played against their number six, he kicked me really hard.'

'My mum and dad are in the crowd – I don't want to mess up in front of them.'

'I'm still feeling down as a result of my cat's death.'

'I don't think I'll last 90 minutes . . . not as young as I used to be.'

'I can't run around when it's hot.'

'They're better than we are. We're bound to lose.'

'Maybe next year, Ges.'

'When we've trained more. Not today.'

Gerry looked around, staring at each face in turn. He opened his mouth to speak, but no words came out. He was speechless. Who wouldn't be?

One man against eleven. Ridiculous. Unimaginable. Yet what about the body of Christ, the Church? Each member is vital. Each member needs to play their part. How sad, how strange, and how serious the consequences when we don't . . .

Read 1 Corinthians 12

Q What is the Church described as?
A

Q Why is the Church described like this?
A

Q Why do you think each member is important?
A

Q What do you feel your role is at church?
A

Q In what kinds of ways can you contribute to Church life?
A

Any comments on what you've read:

Any questions you'd like to ask:

Unit 9

What is the Bible?

Dear Jake,

Thanks for writing to me again. I enjoyed the story of 'The Team'. It's a good job football teams don't behave like that. Can you just picture it – Manchester United turning out to play with only two players! It would be ridiculous. So I think I understood the point. Church is important and it's like being part of a team with your own part to play. The only problem is Mum's not keen to go to church again. She says she feels 'a flush of embarrassment' every time she thinks about it. I am trying to find a good church to go to. I am not sure that the church Mum and I went to fits with the list you gave me. When I find a new church, I'll let you know. I do know it's important and haven't forgotten what you said.

Jake, I wonder if you can help me because once again I'm a little confused. Well a lot confused actually. It's all about the . . . well let me explain right from the beginning.

It all began in morning assembly. Mondays are always whole-school assemblies so we were practising our sardines-in-a-tin impression. You know what I mean, squashed so close to the people next to you that not only can you smell what they had for breakfast, but you can see it on their teeth! Sorry for being gross but it's true.

Normally assemblies are times to catch up on things I've missed, like sleep. The older you get, the more practised you become in the art. Sleeping without slouching, sleeping without snoring and finally when you are elevated into master class, sleeping with your eyes open. Some of the fifth formers have managed this superior skill. You can see them sitting unflinching, unblinking with their eyes glazed. It's not easy, it takes years of practice; I am still a novice at the moment.

But you get the picture: Monday morning, teacher droning, me beginning to sleep. That's when it happened, that's when a few words spoken hit me like a thunderbolt. That's when I jumped up in my chair and started a domino effect which meant that poor Billy Bigalow went flying off his seat. He was sitting on the end of our row. Poor lad landed with an awful thud. He let out a yell, everyone around him started laughing, apart from the teachers who were trying to keep everyone quiet.

What had startled me so much was what the deputy head had said: 'The Bible is not worth the paper it is printed on.'

Why did it have such an effect on me? I don't know. Why did I feel everyone was looking at me? I don't know. They were all busy staring at Billy Bigalow who was nursing his elbow and whimpering. 'The Bible is not worth the paper it is printed on.' Those words kept spinning round my head like a plate on a stick. (You know – like the ones you see on 'The Generation Game'.)

After the school assembly I saw the deputy head going to the school notice board. After he had pinned something on it and walked away, I decided to investigate.

'The Bible is not worth the paper it is printed on'. School debate, Friday the 17th, 3:30pm. All welcome. The debating team will be representing the above statement. That last sentence sent shock waves the size of tidal waves through me. Everyone knew that the debating team had graduated to university at birth, but I knew they were wrong about the Bible, right, Jake? I really want them to be proved wrong but what can I do? I don't know how to debate. I don't even know what to say but something inside of me says I should go. Is that God do you think? If it is, then he's really going to have to help me, and you too, Jake, please. Pretty please with peanut butter on.

Yours panickingly,

Sam

Dear Sam,

Sardines in a tin! Pushing people off their chairs in assembly! I thought you would have learned your lesson after going to church: remember the lady with the hat? It's a good job you kept awake on camp or goodness knows what damage you would have done. I have visions of the whole PA system coming crashing down because you have slipped into the land of slumber and slid off your chair and onto the mixing desk!

Sorry, Sam, I am only joking. Hope you don't mind but I do find your letters contain a certain amount of humour.

What you wrote about and asked me about is a very big issue. The Bible is the Word of God. It changes people's lives today. Is it true? Yes. Is it accurate? Yes. Is it worth the paper it is written on? You'd better believe it!

I have enclosed some notes for you to look at and a sketch. I hope that you find them helpful.

Sam, when you said you felt like you ought to go even though you didn't want to go, I do believe that was God speaking to you. Remember the Holy Spirit? One of the things he does is to convict us. Speak to us in a very clear way. Lots of times I have been scared to speak out about God but every time I have opened my mouth and spoken out God has helped me and given me the words. Sam, it is up to you whether you go to the debate but I will be praying for you.

Yours prayingly,

Jake

PS Remember, God answers prayer.

PPS Please don't shove the debating team on the floor like poor Billy Bigalow!

Brainless, boring or best-seller?

Is the Bible a waste of space? Is it a book not worth using our intellect on? Is it the dullest, daftest material in existence? Or is it a life changing, life enhancing, life fulfilling book?

Take your pick because the Bible falls into one of the above categories. Some people believe the Bible to be boring. Some think it is not worth the paper it is printed on and others find it has the power to radically change their lives.

Why does the Bible court so much publicity and controversy? What is the truth about the world's number one best selling book?

Let us look at the Bible and examine the evidence.

What is the Bible?

To call the Bible a book is in one sense correct and in another sense an inaccurate picture of what the Bible actually is. The Bible is a library of books. Sixty-six in total, divided into two main parts: the Old Testament (containing 39 books), and the New Testament (containing 27 books). The Old Testament charts the history of the Jewish nation and the New Testament chronicles the life of Jesus and the birth of the Christian Church. The main theme and story running throughout the whole Bible is of God's salvation for humankind.

Who wrote the Bible?

It is estimated that the Bible was written over a period of approximately 4000 years. That's a long time for anyone to write a book! So it may not come as a surprise to you that it was written by many different people. A very diverse group too . . . kings, shepherds, poets, priests, fishermen, politicians. All types of people in all walks of life. The main point to grasp is that although the writers were different, the author was the same. God is the one who inspired the people who wrote the book, his book, his story. Someone once said that 'history' was really 'his story'.

How do we know that God is the inspiration behind the Bible? Simple. The Bible tells us.

ALL Scripture is GOD-breathed and is USEFUL for TEACHING, REBUKING, CORRECTING and TRAINING in RIGHTEOUSNESS (2 Timothy 3:16).

Is the Bible accurate?

Many people disclaim the Bible, saying that it is inaccurate and cannot be relied upon.

I wonder if those people realise that the New Testament is the most historically proven document there is!

Two of the tests laid down by historians are:

1. How many manuscripts exist?
2. What is the time span between when they were written and when the events actually took place?

If for example there is only one written work about an event, and the writing was done a thousand years after the event took place, there wouldn't be much credibility to the historical accuracy of the document.

- The New Testament was written between AD 40 and AD 100.
- The earliest copy we have is AD 130 (full manuscripts AD 350).
- Time span of 399 years.
- Number of copies – 5,000 Greek; 10,000 Latin and 9,300 others.

To compare that to any other historical document, the closest is Livy's Roman history written between 59 BC and AD 17; earliest copy AD 900; time span of 900 years. Number of copies 20.

A remarkable difference. You cannot argue with facts!

Why is the Bible unique?

God wrote the book!

That alone makes the Bible a rather special and unique book. There may be many classic books around but the Bible is the only one written by God. As a result of this fact the Bible has a remarkable power to transform people's lives.

Once again listen to what the Bible says:

For the word of God is living and active. Sharper than any double-edged sword, it penetrates even to dividing soul and spirit, joints and marrow; it judges the thoughts and attitudes of the heart. Hebrews 4:12

Millions of lives have been radically changed by the power of God's Word. No other book can stake such a claim.

Out of the frying pan

Characters
OM *Old man in the Wild West; a little crazed.*
YC *Young cowboy*
[Play both characters with exaggerated Wild West accents]

Scene
The old man stands looking up and down the landscape. He takes a deep breath and sniffs the air. He takes his shoes and socks off and rolls up his trouser legs. Turning round he picks up a frying pan and steps into the river. As he is bending down with his frying pan, a young cowboy enters the scene.

YC Howdy!

The man with the frying pan makes no response

YC Howdy!

Still no response

YC HOWDY, OLD-TIMER!

This time the man with the frying pan jumps out of his skin and clutches his heart

OM What ya think ya doin'? Nearly scared me out of me rabbit boots.

YC You ain't wearin' no rabbit boots.

Old man looks down

OM If I had been wearing rabbit boots I would have jumped plumb out of 'em.

YC What ya doin'?

OM What does it look like I'm a-doin'?

YC Frying an egg?

OM Nope.

YC Scrambling an egg?

OM Nope.

YC Fishing with a frying pan?

OM Nope.

YC Takin' your frying pan for a swim?

OM Nope.

YC Well, ya got me goat then.

OM What's that kind of talk . . . 'got me goat'?

YC I have Scottish grandparents.

OM Oh.

YC So, what ya doin'?

The old man looks around, turns back, opens his eyes really wide (in a very crazed way), beckons the young man to come nearer. Thinking he is going to whisper a big secret, the young man leans forward, turning his head sideways so that his ear is close to the old man

OM GOLD!!

The word is shouted into the young man's ear, who jumps back

YC What ya yellin' and hollerin' for old man? I ain't deaf, ya know!

OM GOLD!!!!!

YC I heard ya the first time. Now calm down or you'll be swallowin' your teeth.

OM Wouldn't be the first time.

YM There ain't no gold in these here hills.

OM I ain't looking in the hills.

YC There ain't no gold in this here river.

OM   Says who?

YC   Says me. How long ya been looking?

OM   A while.

YC   What's a while? A day? A week? A month? A year?

OM   Forty-two years, two hundred and twenty-one days, seven hours and fifteen minutes.

YC   Ya plum tooting crazy ol'-timer! Now get ya self outta that freezing stream and come into town.

OM   Nope.

YC   It'll be your funeral!!

OM   It's me fortune!

YC   You're welcome to it all.

The young cowboy shakes his head and walks off. The old man watches him go, then bends down again with his frying pan. A few shakes and he picks something up. Looks at it. Looks at the man walking away and smiles

OM   Gold! (*Said in a very hushed tone*).

The Bible is the word of God. In his word, God tells us about searching out wisdom:

Search for it like silver, and hunt for it like hidden treasure. Then you will understand and know respect for the Lord, and you will find that you know God. Proverbs 2:4-5

The Bible is worth digging into. Spend some time searching and hunting, and you will discover the depths of God's riches!

Read Psalm 1 and Psalm 119:89-105

Q What does the psalmist delight in?
A

Q Why is that his delight?
A

Q How does God's word help him?
A

Q How does God's word help you?
A

Q Why is God's word a light to our path?
A

Any comments on what you've read:

Any questions you'd like to ask:

Unit 10

How do you read the Bible?

Dear Jake,

Thanks for your letter. I never knew the Bible was so historical. Accurate and all that I mean. It blew my mind. Not literally! You know what I am saying.

The debate is four days away. I am starting to get very nervous. Yesterday at school I bumped into one of the debating team. I knew he was one of the team because he always walks around school carrying encyclopaedias. Big, thick, heavy ones. They go right up to his nose. Or at least that's where they used to perch until I bumped into him. After that collision they were scattered all over the school corridor.

'You shouldn't run in the corridor.'

How do you know I was running, you had your head in your books.'

'The velocity at which your body impacted with mine allied with the angle at which you pole-axed me would substantiate my verdict of events.'

'Eh?' It was the only thing I could think of to say.

'You ran in to me.'

'So I did. So I am sorry. Can I help pick your books up?'

'If you had followed the correct school policy and procedures, set off for class at the exact moment for the necessary class, walking on the right side of the corridor, moving at a speed conducive to someone not in a hurry, then this unfortunate incident need never have taken place.'

'So do you want me to help or not?'

'Due to the fact that we are now both precisely fifty-three seconds late for class I recommend that we collect my reading material at the fastest pace our hands will allow.'

'Is that a Yes?'

'Affirmative.'

As I began to pick up some of his books a piece of paper fell from the pages. I quickly scooped it up and saw the heading. 'Notes for school debate. The Bible is not worth the paper it is printed on.' There were reams and reams of notes. It was A4-sized paper and it was full on both sides! I was shocked. I was panicking. I was feeling like a jelly on a plate. I handed him his books back and without a word he disappeared down the corridor leaving me all alone and shaking inside.

That night when I went home I decided to do some study of my own. I went to my bedroom, picked up my Bible, sat down and began to read. Genesis, that was the first book of the Bible, so I thought I would start there. Start in Genesis and read all the way right through from cover to cover.

It must have been late when Mum came into the room. The glare of the street lights penetrated the window. Mum just smiled when she saw me, took the Bible off my lap and said: 'Bedtime now, Samuel, goodnight and God bless.'

I crawled into bed and tried to remember what I had read. Nothing. My mind was a blank. I had no idea how many pages I had read before I fell asleep but I had remembered nothing. Jake, what am I going to do? How do you read the Bible? How do you make sense of it all? Can you write to me quickly, please.

Yours, even more panickingly,

Sam

Dear Sam,

What a guy you are! Disturbing assemblies, knocking hats off old ladies and now this, sending someone sprawling in the school corridor! Whatever next? I dread to think! One thing is for certain, your life is not dull. Sorry to ramble on but I do find your escapades very interesting.

Back to the issue at hand. The debate is only a few days away and you're beginning to feel slightly nervous about the whole proceedings. I do feel for you, Sam. Looking at the situation in human terms it does look very daunting. The good news is that God is part of the equation, a major part! Remember, God has promised never to leave or forsake us. We may not always be aware of his presence but he is there and he does care.

How to read the Bible. How to understand it. Very big questions – I admire your zeal in trying to read through the whole Bible in one night! However, as you have discovered, that is not the best way to read the Bible. Enclosed are some notes and more information about the Bible. I do pray that they will be of use to you.

Yours prayingly,

Jake

PS Please try not to pole-axe any more of the debating team. I think you can win fair and square!

How not to read the Bible

Cast
Narrator who reads the lines
Actor who acts out what has been described

N   There are various ways of reading the Bible.

        A stands up and holds out the Bible

N   You can read it upside down.

        A turns the Bible upside down and tries to read it

N   We do not recommend this approach. You may go cross-eyed, feel dizzy or be looked upon as a gibbering loony.

        A stops reading the Bible that way

N   You can read it from the end to the beginning.

        A opens the Bible, says 'Amen' and then closes it again

N   You can read the Bible backwards.

        A opens the Bible and starts to read a verse as follows:

        'Amen, people God's with be Jesus Lord the of grace The'

N   You can read the words backwards.

        A opens the Bible and attempts to read the words backwards

N   You can read the Bible at random.

        A says, 'He who digs a hole and scoops it out falls into the pit he has made. A fool's work wearies him. He does not know the way to turn.'

N   You can read bits from different books.

        A starts reading out odd words

N   We do not recommend these ways as they are rather confusing and stupid!

        A exclaims: 'So how do you read the Bible?'

Reading and feeding

So . . . how *should* you read the Bible? Reading it backwards, standing on your head, or reading at random is not very helpful. So where do you begin?

Remember the library?

You have just entered a huge room. Lights hang low from the ceiling, illuminating the contents standing before you. Row upon row of books. Your eyes spin as you are dazzled by the sight of so many volumes of print. You only came for one book to help with your history homework. Slowly you shuffle towards the first bookcase, pick up the first paperback on the shelf and start to read the title: *How To Grow Tomatoes In Sub-zero Temperatures* by Arctic Arthur.

The book is not the one you were looking for. With a deep sigh you place it back on the shelf and your fingers reach out for the next book. Something tells you it's going to be a long day . . .

Stop!

Freeze!

Rewind the tape. That is not what you would do! Not in a million, trillion, zillion years. If you went to a library for a book you would go to the right section. To find a history book, you would go to the history section. The books are listed alphabetically. There are other guides to help you choose the book you want. Fiction or non-fiction, what period of history. Not to forget that there are library assistants who are there to help!

The Bible is God's library. It is filled with a wide variety of books. Some are historical, some composed of poetry, some are letters, some are allegories.

What's that you're reading?

There are nine distinct categories that the Bible is divided into:
Old Testament
- History
- Law
- Prophecy

- Poetry
- Wisdom

New Testament
- Gospels
- Acts
- Letters
- Revelation

It is of vital importance that when you pick up the Bible and begin flicking through the pages you realise what type of book you are reading. Your *understanding* and *interpretation* of the Bible will be greatly helped when you know what it is you're reading!

How to make the Bible speak to your soul

- Read it! Basic but true. Many people believe in the Bible but don't open its cover. Don't be one of them.

- Find a good time of day to read. A time when you are awake! A time when you are undisturbed.

- Discipline. Get into the habit of reading the Bible.

- Find relevant Bible notes to help you understand.

- Pray and ask God to speak to you through his word. He will!

Read 2 Timothy 3:16 and Hebrews 4:12

Q How much of God's word is useful?
A

Q Why is the Bible unique?
A

Q What is your favourite verse in the Bible?
A

Q What helps you understand the Bible?
A

Q Why is just reading the Bible not enough?
A

Any comments on what you've read:

Any questions you'd like to ask:

Unit 11

What is prayer?

Dear Jake,

What a week I've had. You would never believe it. Well, I hope you will believe it because what I am going to tell you is the truth. Like all good stories I'll start at the beginning, although this isn't a story! Here goes.

I hardly slept a wink the night before the school debate. After receiving your letter I tried to put your advice into practice. Problem was I didn't have much time and I could feel the panic rising, almost choking me.

When morning came, I could hardly open my eyes. Mum kept shouting at me to get up but I could hardly turn in my bed, never mind stand. Eventually she burst into my room, screaming in a very high-pitched voice, the words bounced off the bedroom walls but didn't land on me. She flung open the curtains and sunlight streaked into the room stinging my eyes.

'Mum!' I croaked.

'Samuel. It's time to get up. You'll be late for school . . . and it's your big debate today.'

For a split-second I had forgotten. For a few blissful moments it had not been on my mind. Now it was pouring in like a flood. The big debate. Today. Me against the whole universe or at least the school debating team which amounted to the same thing.

'Time to get up Samuel . . . Now!'

'Mum, I . . .'

I thought of a thousand excuses, none of which would stand up under Mum's cross-examination (and it would be cross).

'. . . I'm getting up, now.'

'Good,' said Mum and she slammed the door shut behind her.

I think she was upset.

Trudging to school that morning I didn't know what to do. My imagination began playing weird scenes, pictures of me walking into the debate and a gallows hanging there. Or pictures of the debating team's faces pushed into mine.

'So you're the one person in the school who believes the Bible.'

'You're the one boy in the country who believes it's true.'

'You're the only one on the planet who reads the Book.'

Then all the faces started laughing, their faces growing larger and larger and the laughter becoming hysterical. The pictures and images filled my mind. I couldn't shake them off. I couldn't shift them. I didn't know what to do. So I slapped myself, a right-hander right on my face. That stopped the thoughts. My cheek was stinging but it put a stop to my nightmare. As I was standing rubbing my face I noticed a gang of first-years watching me. They must have witnessed the whole scene. Watched me walking down the road, then suddenly strike my own face.

I pretended I had just swatted a fly that had been bothering me, gave them a hard stare then walked off.

I was acting like a complete idiot even before I got to school. What could I do? I was feeling desperate. I was feeling deep despair. I was desperately despairing of dying at school that day. What could I do?

Jake, I prayed. Not something I'm good at or do often but it was the only thing I could think of. A very short and simple prayer that went along the lines of: 'Help . . . . Please help . . . please, please, please, God . . . help!'

Turning into Orchard Drive I could see our school building. I could see the school gates and I could see . . . fire engines. Two of them standing boldly in front of the main entrance. There were lots of firefighters running in and out of the building. Some teachers were standing near the engines and . . . this was the amazing bit, turning, yes, actually turning people away. I couldn't believe my eyes. Yes, I could believe in the fire engines being at the school –

but teachers refusing pupils entrance to school? I never thought I would live to see the day.

What had happened, Jake, was some faulty electrical wiring had caused a fire on the top floor. Fortunately the caretaker was quick to notice some smoke and before much damage could be done the fire brigade were there. School had to be closed for three days whilst everything was sorted out.

Jake, did I make the school burn down? Was that God's answer to my prayer? I dare not pray again. Who knows what damage I could do?

Any advice, Jake?

Yours, very confusedly,

Sam

Dear Sam,

What a letter. What a life. What can I say?

You say a prayer, the school burns down. Is there a connection? Errm! Good question Sam. I have had to pray about this one a lot myself.

Firstly, God does answer prayer. That is a fact that we can depend on. Secondly, God doesn't always answer our prayers in the way which we would expect.

Thirdly, God is not in the habit of destroying things by fire!

There have been many times I have prayed for God's help and received it in lots of different ways and whilst God is not limited in what he can do, he does work within certain parameters. God is a God of love. The Bible tells us clearly that God is love. Although we live in a world of pain and suffering God is not the one who intentionally inflicts them on us. Remember sin? Remember its consequences.

Whilst I could never second-guess everything God is going to do, I do believe it would be totally out of his character to burn schools down on the whim of one of his children.

To understand prayer we need to understand God more. Sam, I hope my notes on prayer do help. I will be praying for you, Sam.

Yours prayingly,

Jake

Relationship or ritual?

The phone rings but you don't answer. There is a knock on the door but you don't go. An envelope drops through the letter box and remains unopened.

Your best friend keeps on trying to communicate with you. Time after time they approach your house. They stand on the doorstep ringing the bell, they knock as loud as they can but always remain on the outside looking in.

Your best friend is kept waiting in the wings. Your best friend? A friend that you don't speak to on the phone, a friend that you don't open the door to, a friend whose letters you don't open. What kind of friendship is that?

Good friends, real friends spend time together; quality time. They share their lives with one another. They open their hearts to one another. They know each other. Friendship is about relating to someone. It is about relationship.

The Christian life is not about simply following a set of rules, it is about being in a personal relationship with the living God.

Prayer is talking to God. It is our primary way of sharing, of speaking, of communicating with him. From the depths of our heart, to the thoughts on our mind, from our secrets to our desires, from our past to our present to our future hope, prayer is our way of opening up our lives and laying them before God. Prayer is not a set language, or something set out in stone, it is setting out ourselves and all that we are to God.

If we take a peek into the Psalms we can see the rich variety of situations in which the psalmist prayed.

When he was in **trouble**
Psalm 142:1-2
I cry aloud to the Lord, I lift up my voice to the Lord for mercy. I pour out my complaint before him; before him I tell my trouble.

When he was **upset**
Psalm 137:1
By the rivers of Babylon we sat and wept when we remembered Zion.

When he needed **help**
Psalm 140:1
Rescue me, O Lord, from evil men; protect me from men of violence.

When he was **happy**
Psalm 145:1
I will exalt you, my God the King; I will praise your name for ever and ever.

When he needed **security**
Psalm 125:1
Those who trust in the Lord are like Mount Zion, which cannot be shaken but endures for ever.

When he needed **provision**
Psalm 23:1
The Lord is my shepherd, I shall not be in want.

When he needed **rest**
Psalm 23:2
He makes me lie down in green pastures, he leads me beside quiet waters.

When he needed **forgiveness**
Psalm 51:2
Wash away all my iniquity and cleanse me from my sin.

When he needed **instruction**
Psalm 112:1
Praise the Lord. Blessed is the man who fears the Lord, who finds great delight in his instruction.

When he needed **mercy**
Psalm 116:5
The Lord is gracious and righteous; our God is full of compassion.

How wonderful that whatever we are feeling and whatever we are doing we can talk to God.

Snakes for supper

It is late in the evening, time for bed, time to rest your weary head. Yet before you climb the stairs, before you enter the land of slumber, you have a job to do. You need to answer an urgent enquiry, or rather a demand. It is coming from the area of your stomach. The message it is sending: Feed me!

You know it is late. You know you shouldn't eat but your body is convincing you otherwise.

'Dad?'

'Yes, son?'

'Can I have something to eat?'

'It's late.'

'I'm very hungry.'

'OK.'

'Thanks, Dad.'

A few minutes later your dad reappears with a plate containing a slippery, slimy, slithering . . . snake! Your dad pops it on your lap and says:

'Enjoy.'

You throw the plate in the air and scream the house down!

Ever had that experience? No? I am not surprised! What father would give his son a snake to eat if he was hungry?

> *Which of you, if his son asks him for bread, will give him a stone? Or if he asks for a fish, will give him a snake? If you, then, though you are evil, know how to give good gifts to your children, how much more will your Father in heaven give good gifts to those who ask him!*
> Matthew 7:9-11

When we ask God, he will never give us anything that will harm us. Not a stone or a snake or a smouldering school! God only gives good gifts because God is good.

Read Matthew 6:5-15

Q How does Jesus tell us to pray?
A

Q How should we NOT pray?
A

Q What does God know before we pray?
A

Q What does the Lord's Prayer teach us?
A

Q Why do you think Jake decided it was not God that set Sam's school on fire?
A

Any comments on what you've read:

Any questions you'd like to ask:

Unit 12

How do you pray?

Dear Jake,

I'm bored. I thought school was boring, but being stuck at home is even more boring. The problems the fire caused were worse than they first thought. So a few days off school is now turning into over a week! They say school will be re-opened soon. I will have forgotten what it looks like by then. I am bored!

Thanks for your letter on prayer. It did help me. I no longer think I am responsible for the fire just because I prayed I didn't want to go to school that day.

Being off school with nothing much to do, I decided to go for a walk. I nipped through town and headed out towards the river. It was one of those rare days in summer. The sun was shining. We've had nothing but rain followed by more rain up here for weeks. I hope that the weather is going to be good on camp again this summer; it was red hot last year. I can't wait for camp, it's only a few months away now. Sorry to ramble, Jake, but like I said, I am bored.

Back to the river. It's pleasant down by the river bank, especially on a nice day in summer. On a weekend you see lots of families picnicking. Well, this was midweek and there was hardly anyone around. I saw one old guy sitting fishing. I could see him from a distance and the closer I got the more I thought, is he real or is he a big gnome placed by the riverside by a garden centre? The man never moved. I wondered if I got really close to him whether I might see him blink or twitch or flinch or budge or breathe or do something. I even dared to stand right behind him. There was still no movement. I thought about saying something but couldn't think of anything more original to say than 'hello' so I didn't bother. What I did do was plonk myself on the bank just above where he was sitting. I thought I could watch him fish and . . . this is the part were you are going to be really impressed . . . pray! Yes, pray.

So I perched myself on the grass, put my hands together, closed my eyes, bowed my head and prayed, and prayed and payed . . . for hours. Or at least that's what happened in my dreams. What really happened was that I did start to pray but found myself nodding off. The more I tried to pray the more I could feel my head dropping onto my chest. I wish I had stopped then and carried on walking or at least stayed awake. What made me open my eyes was the noise – the noise of a large, big splash! When I looked I realised that it wasn't a gnome sitting with a fishing rod but a real man because he was the one making all the noise splashing about in the river. He was coughing and spluttering.

I didn't know what to do. I must have fallen asleep, rolled down the hill and bumped into the man, sending him flying. It was all accidental stuff, I am sure he would understand but I didn't stay around long enough to find out. Sorry to say that I legged it, but I did.

Now, not only dare I not go back to the river but I hardly dare pray. How do you stay awake when you pray? How do you know God's listening? How long should you pray for? How do you know God answers?

Just a few questions from a very bored teenager.
Yours boringly,

Sam

Dear Sam,

ZZZ ZZZ ZZZ . . .

Sorry, Sam, I was just praying or should I say sleeping! What a letter! What a corking story! What will be the next adventure of Sam, boy wonder, extraordinary hero of our times? I can't wait to see the film version of your life. It certainly will make fascinating viewing!

In your letter you did ask a lot of very good questions. They seemed to cover a wide range of issues on prayer from practical to spiritual. Once again, I thought the best way to try to answer them was by some notes, with a little drama sketch thrown in too. Hope that you enjoy them. I do hope that you manage to stay awake whilst reading them! Sorry, Sam, I must apologise for my sense of humour but you do make it difficult for me. I am going to be very careful the next time I walk by the river, I never know who might be rolling down the hill towards me!

Yours entertainedly,

Jake

PS I hope that the weather will be good on camp too.
PPS I am looking forward to camp as well.

Practical and spiritual points on prayer

When do we talk to people?

All the time. In various places and in different ways. We talk to our friends walking to school, our family at home, the bus driver as we climb on board, our teachers in lessons, the people who work in shops, our long-distance relatives on the phone. Speech and conversation are part of everyday life.

When can we talk to God?

All the time. In various places and in different ways. We can talk to him on our way to school, at home, in class, in the shops, in the park, when by the river! God is always there. God is always listening, so we can share with him about anything and everything.

How do you talk to God?

In all kinds of ways. We don't have to close our eyes, put our hands together or bow our heads, although this may help. We don't have to speak out loud. We don't have to speak for a long time. We can pray for others, for our own needs, for the world, or our future. We can talk and share because God is there and God does . . . really does care.

Here are a few words of encouragement from the Bible to help us pray:

Cast all your anxiety on him because he cares for you. 1 Peter 5:7

Do not be anxious about anything, but in everything, present your requests to God. And the peace of God, which transcends all under-standing, will guard your hearts and your minds in Christ Jesus. Philippians 4:6-7

God wants to hear our hurts, desires to listen about our disappointments, longs to learn of our lives, all our hopes, aspirations, needs, fears, thoughts, every single thing.

God is not a fickle friend or a passing stranger but a permanent resident in our lives. He wants us to feel at home with him.

So, does God always answer our prayers? Yes! But answering is not the same as allowing. What do I mean by that? Because God loves us, he wants the best for us.

I have a son who is one year old. He has his own ways of communicating with us. He has little hands that want to touch everything, grab everything. As a parent I have to watch him carefully. He needs protection. Protecting from himself sometimes. As a parent I will try to ensure he is cared for, looked after and loved.

God, in his love and wisdom will not always give us what we ask for but what we need.

Sometimes God may answer our prayers by saying 'no' or 'not now' or 'yes'. We need to trust that God knows best, and as a perfect parent God does.

For the last words on prayer I will leave you with the words of Jesus.

Ask and it will be given to you;
seek and you will find;
knock and the door will be opened to you.
For everyone who asks receives;
he who seeks finds;
and to him who knocks,
the door will be opened.
Matthew 7:7-8

Persistence pays off!

Scene
A man walks onto the stage, looks up, smiles, stretches his arms and sighs deeply.

Man   What a lovely day. The sun is shining, the flowers blooming, and the clouds non-existent. What a perfect day. Work was . . . rewarding. (*Brings out a bag full of coins*) If a job's worth doing, it's worth doing profitably. What a wonderful day. What could possibly go wrong?

Enter woman clutching a piece of paper in her hand. She is busy reading and doesn't see the man. He smiles, head held high, turns and bumps into the woman. Piece of paper falls to the floor. Both go to pick it up. The man gets there first. Standing up, he gives it to the woman.

Man   My dear lady, I am so terribly . . . *(He looks up and sees who it is)* You . . . you . . . you . . . not you!

Woman   Yes, it's me.

Man   What are you doing here?

Woman   What do you think?

Man   What is this? *(Points to paper)*

Woman   What do you think?

Man   It's not?

Woman   It is.

Man looks disgustedly at paper, pulls a face

Woman   Go on. Read it. Do something about it.

Man   I can't. Not now. I said so. Told you, many times.

Woman   Your answerphone told me.

Man   I wrote and told you.

Woman   Your secretaries did.

Man   You kept on writing.

Woman   Three hundred and nine times to be precise.

Man   You kept phoning.

Woman   Seven hundred and twenty-one times.

Man   I had to unplug the fax machine.

Woman   And you stopped me coming into your office.

Man   I hope it didn't hurt too much when they threw you out.

Woman   What do you care?

Man   Well, I don't actually.

Woman   Exactly. You don't care about me or justice. You don't care about the poor or the widows, only money. That's all you care about.

Man	It's close to my heart.
Woman	It's a millstone around your neck.
Man	Look. Will you please leave me alone?
Woman	No.
Man	Please, no more letters, phone calls, faxes. OK?
Woman	No.
Man	But why?
Woman	Because I want justice and you are the judge.
	Man paces up and down, acts annoyed and exasperated
Man	You – you – you'll get what you asked for. I'll hear your case. I'll listen to all you have to say. Justice will be done.
Woman	YES! *(Jumps in the air)*
Man	Please calm down, this is a respectable neighbourhood. Now good day.
Woman	Good day.

Take a look at this story as told by Jesus in Luke 18:1-8. What impact does this have on the way you pray?

Read Luke 11:1-13

Q What does this parable teach us?
A

Q Why should we not give up when we pray?
A

Q What gives us the confidence to go to God BOLDLY in prayer?
A

Q How will God respond to our prayers?
A

Q What advice would you give to Sam about praying?
A

Any comments on what you've read:

Any questions you'd like to ask:

Unit 13

What is evangelism?

Dear Jake,

Hooray! School's restarted. Went back yesterday and it was great, I really enjoyed it. No, of course I'm not ill! I was very bored at home, that's all. There's nothing wrong with enjoying school, is there?

The good news was that the school debate, you know the one on 'The Bible not being worth the paper it is printed on' has been cancelled!! Too much work for people to catch up on, so they said. I know the real reason, they were afraid of losing. After all, no one would have stood a chance against my wisdom and wit! Modest little chap, aren't I?

Jake, now that I'm back at school there's something I really want to do. Tell people about Jesus. I hope you were sitting down when you read that bit! It's true though, I really do. I know I've been a chicken in the past, I know I was really scared about the debate but I know this is something really important that I want to do. After your last letter I decided to try and spend some time praying. I managed to stay awake all the time too, pretty amazing for me, don't you think?

When I was talking to God I decided to do what the psalmist did, tell God just how I felt. So I talked and I talked and I kept talking for ages. Went on about being bored, about school, my family, even my pet goldfish, Lobster (you don't think Lobster is a funny name for a goldfish do you? My dad thinks it's stupid) and about my friends. That's when it struck me. None of my friends are Christians. Not one of them. So when I talked to God about them I started asking him to help them become Christians. I didn't know how he was going to do it but this is the weird part because a few hours later I was reading my Bible. I hope you're taking careful note of all this, Mr Youth Leader. Is pride a sin? Anyway, I was reading this bit in the Bible and it sprang out at me. Not literally, I mean the words didn't fly off the paper and splat me in the face or anything, but the words did hit me hard, not on my face but inside my head. This is what I read: 'Everyone who calls on the name of the Lord will be saved. How, then, can they call on the one they have not believed in? And how can they believe in the one of whom they have not heard? And how can they hear without someone preaching to them?'

I read it and read it and read it. It made so much sense. How can people believe in someone they haven't heard about? How can they hear unless someone tells them?

The thoughts kept spinning round in my head. What about my friends at school? Who's told them? Has anyone told them? Should I tell them? How can I tell them?

Since I read these verses in the Bible, I've had a few thoughts on how to tell people about Jesus. Please tell me what you think.

1. Walk up and down the estate with one of those big sandwich boards on declaring 'Jesus loves you', or 'Get on board with the Lord'.
2. Shout through people's letterboxes the message of love and forgiveness.
3. Hijack the local radio station and make them read the whole Bible over the air waves.
4. Stick Bible tracts in all my classmates' school books.
5. Write John 3:16 on all the boards at school.
6. Stand in the school yard at break and begin preaching.
7. Walk round the school corridors chanting Bible verses.
8. Always include a scripture in my homework.
9. Ask all the Christians in the town to come with me to school and tell everyone about Jesus.
10. Stand on the school fields and yell at the top of my voice.

You tell people about Jesus, Jake. What do you think?

Yours evangelisingly,

Sam

Dear Sam,

Or should I say, 'Billy Graham'? You do sound like a budding evangelist. I am thrilled and encouraged to hear about your love and concern for your friends, and you are quite right about your responsibility to tell them. What to do next? That is the big question.

I remember when I was a similar age to you – yes, I have got a good memory and can remember that far back! I had been a Christian for a few months and began to have an overwhelming burden to tell people about Jesus. What could or should I do?

What I did was share how I felt with one of the church leaders who was very wise and very caring. He listened to me, prayed with me and gave me a book called 'I Believe in Evangelism' by David Watson. The book was very helpful.

A few weeks later someone in the church came to talk with me. I didn't really know this person, only by sight, but he strongly felt that God had been talking to him about me! Sounds scary but it was wonderful. The word 'evangelist' was what was on his heart.

I was bowled over. Gobsmacked. What now? Rush into the streets and tell everyone, go into the market square and proclaim the gospel?

What I did was to talk to my friends and family. Not to preach at them but to share with them. People who knew me and people who had seen the changes in me since I had become a Christian.

Sam, I don't know if God is calling you to be an evangelist. He might be! What I do know is that every Christian is a witness of Jesus Christ and has a responsibility to share with others. To try to help you understand I have enclosed some notes. I do really hope they are helpful.

Yours likewise evangelisingly,

Jake

A witness . . . for what?

The room is hushed in silence. A gallery of people gather to hear the evidence and discover the verdict. Central players in the drama that is about to unfold stand to attention as the judge strides into court.

Now the cast is assembled, the action is about to begin. A witness is called to the box. Their evidence crucial to the case in question. Whilst the formal introductions are dispensed with, the air of anticipation filters through the room. What will this person say? What facts will be revealed? What evidence will be unearthed?

A wigged lawyer approaches the person in the witness box. The lawyer stands calm, composed, cool and collected, prepared to do battle for his client, prepared to examine and cross examine the witness, prepared to expose any flaws in the evidence about to be given.

Lawyer   You are Mr Carsdale of Number 10, Ploddington Place?

All eyes are on Mr Carsdale in the witness box. No one turns away as they watch the response and the reaction of the man being questioned. There is a long pause, so long that the lawyer feels compelled to speak.

Lawyer   You are Mr Fredrick Bartholomew Cuthbert Carsdale of Number 10, Ploddington Place?

The man in the box shuffles his feet and nervously chews his fingernails.

Lawyer   Mr Carsdale, are you going to speak today? Are you going to address the court? Are you going to grace us with the use of your vocal chords? Are you going to utter a sound or a syllable? Or are you going to waste our time and the taxpayers' money? Mr Carsdale, what are you going to do?

From anticipation, to expectation, to tension, the atmosphere shifts and changes within the four walls of the court room. The keys to the case are held by the man standing before the jury, but with his mouth locked there will be no enlightenment and no justice dispensed.

Lawyer   Mr Carsdale, I must press you for an answer or ask you to step down. Are you a witness or are you not?

That's a very good question.

Someone once said: 'If you were put on trial for being a Christian, would there be enough evidence to convict you?'

Jesus said to his disciples:

This is what is written: the Christ will suffer and rise from the dead on the third day, and repentance and forgiveness of sins will be preached in his name to all nations, beginning at Jerusalem. You are witnesses of these things. Luke 24:46-48

What Jesus said to his disciples is true for us. If we are Christians, followers of Jesus, and if we know that Jesus died for our sins and rose again, then we are his witnesses. We may not all be evangelists, but we are all witnesses.

What would happen in a court case if someone refused to speak up, refused to tell the truth, refused to give evidence? An innocent person condemned? A guilty one set free? The consequences are drastic and dire. What would the consequences be if we refused to speak to people about Jesus? If we refused to share the truth, refused to give evidence? People might stay condemned under the weight of sin, and guilty people may not realise that they can be pardoned and set free.

A Samaritan, a Saviour and something to share . . .

The day is hot. The road is dusty. The journey is long. The disciples have gone to town in search of food and supplies while Jesus rest himself by a well in the heat of the day. He is tired from his travels.

A woman approaches the well to draw water. Jesus asks her a simple question: 'Will you give me a drink?'

An understandable question given the circumstances. Jesus was tired, he was hot, he had no means of drawing water from the well. The woman had.

What turns the question from being simple to radical are the cultural circumstances of the situation. Jesus was a Jew, the woman was a Samaritan.

Jews and Samaritans did not go to the same parties . . . they did not mix – socially or otherwise. Jesus was a man, the woman was a . . . woman! In the climate of the day this was something else to be frowned upon.

Understanding the background to the dialogue that ensues helps us to see the shock and surprise of the Samaritan woman.

As Jesus engages her in conversation he reveals her need to her. Not a need of mere water, vital as that is to living, but her greater need of living water, which she needs for eternal life.

Both in her questions and in Jesus' answers to her questions, the woman's history is laid open, not in a cold matter-of-fact way but in a caring honest manner.

When Jesus declares who he is, the woman returns to her people telling everyone about him.

This story is found in John 4:1-30. Later on in the same chapter is a very poignant phrase. In verse 39 it states:

Many of the Samaritans from that town believed in him because of the woman's testimony.

She had known Jesus for probably less than one hour, yet her life would never be the same again, and because she had met Jesus she could tell others about him. It wasn't the length of time that was important, it was the personal encounter that was crucial.

We all have our own unique testimony. It does not matter whether we became a Christian when we were 7 or 77, we have our own individual story to share. We may not have all the answers or extensive biblical knowledge but we do know Jesus, and evangelism simply put is 'sharing the good news of Jesus Christ'. If we are Christians we certainly have something to share . . . Christ himself.

Four facets of friendship evangelism

1 Be caring

Care about people. Jesus spoke to a stranger, he didn't have to but he refused to conform to convention and ignore her, instead he cared for her.

We need to care for the people we know and the people that we meet. Take a genuine interest in their lives: don't simply see them as someone else to preach the gospel to.

2 Be honest

Telling the truth isn't always easy. Getting people to face up to reality can be a difficult task. Yet truth is non-negotiable and cannot be watered down or compromised on. If it is, then nobody benefits. Jesus spoke the truth about the woman's private life. Not easy but necessary.

3 Be patient

The Samaritan woman couldn't understand the spiritual truths that Jesus was sharing. He didn't go off in a huff or pack it all in, but patiently continued to share until the penny dropped and the truth dawned.

4 Be there

Be there! We cannot evangelise to Christians! It may sound obvious but you would be amazed how many Christians do this. Hold meetings where only Christians come and then preach the gospel. We need to be where non-Christians are; not always in the places they go to, that is not always a wise or a right move, but we do need to spend time with them. We cannot tell people the good news if we never see them.

Be there for people, be patient as you share, be honest with them, and above all, be able to care, no matter how people respond.

Read Romans 10

Q What was the apostle Paul's prayer?
A

Q Why did Paul pray that prayer?
A

Q How can we share our faith?
A

Q Why is it important to share our faith?
A

Q What advice would you give to Sam?
A

Any comments on what you've read:

Any questions you'd like to ask:

Unit 14

What happens when we let God down?

Dear Jake,

Do you want the bad news or the good news? As Christians we believe in the Good News, so here goes.

After reading your letter I decided it was time to talk with my family. Dad was watching TV and he doesn't like being disturbed but I knew I wanted to tell him. I decided to wait until the adverts came on and then said:

'Dad?'

'Yeah?'

'Um . . . Dad?'

'Yeah?'

'Er . . . Dad?'

'Yes! How much money do you want?'

'No Dad, it's not that.'

'Oh.'

'Do you know God wants to give us eternal life?'

Dad just stared at me. I didn't know what else to say. The programme came back on and Dad turned away but I thought I saw something in his face that was somehow different. Inside I felt really good. I stayed and watched the rest of the programme with Dad.

Feeling really encouraged, I decided it was time to let people know at school that I was a Christian. What I thought would be a good idea was if I went along to the Christian Union group. Show my face, surprise a few people, let them know.

The club meets on a Tuesday, so at lunchtime I set off to the classroom. I was just on my way in through the door when I heard,

'Sammy! Sammy!'

I froze in my tracks and turned my head.

'Sammy! Sammy!'

The loud, rasping sound was coming from Eggo's voice. Eggo is one of those characters that everyone in the school knows, especially the teachers! Eggo got his nickname by sitting in a crate of eggs on a trip to a farm we had in year seven. Ever since then he's been called Eggo – the yoke's on you, don't egg me on and all that kind of stuff.

'Sammy!' Eggo shouted as if I needed reminding of what my name was. I was still standing in my iceberg position. Frozen. Eggo was ambling down the corridor and I could hear the guy inside the classroom talking about Jesus. Everyone inside wasn't listening to him though – they were all staring at me. Not surprising as I had one foot in the class and one foot out.

'Sammy!'

One second I heard my name bellowed in my ear, the next I was sprawled on the classroom floor, all thanks to Eggo's huge shove on my shoulders. People in the classroom erupted in laughter. If that wasn't bad enough, that's when the man said it: 'Are you coming to join us?'

It felt as if someone had turned the heating on full blast. My body thermostat hit the roof. Burning hot cheeks that must have been the colour of beetroot.

'Come on, Sammy, you don't want to listen to someone talking about a dead guy.'

Eggo laughed at what he thought was really funny. Everyone in the class started to look embarrassed apart from the man who looked calm and was smiling at us. 'Are you staying?' he asked again.

'Sammy!' Eggo snorted.

I really wanted to stay, Jake. I really wanted to tell Eggo to shove off and stop being so stupid. I really wanted to tell everyone that I was a Christian. I really did.

'Course I'm not staying!'

I looked around to see who had said those words, but it was my mouth they had popped out from. I walked away. I walked down the corridor with Eggo laughing at all his silly jokes. Why couldn't I stay? Why couldn't I tell him that Jesus was real and he was for everyone?

Sorry to burden you, Jake, but there you have it: I'm a flop, I'm a failure, I knew it all along. I'll never be able to show my face at that Christian Club again. It feels awful to let God down. What can I do now, Jake?

Yours failingly,

Sam

Dear Sam,

Thank you for your letter. Your friend does sound like quite an interesting character. What a nickname! Eggo! He did land you in an awkward situation, literally! In trying to help answer your question I would like to tell you a story of a young man.

This young man had just left college and started his first job. In the tax office. He had not been working there long before he wanted to tell people that he was a Christian but didn't know how. Should he stand singing 'Hallelujah' on top of the desks? Should he hand out a leaflet containing all of the church services in town? What should he do?

One morning he entered the office. Everything seemed as normal. Sounds of people busy at work filled the air. By mid-morning nothing out of the ordinary had happened. It was then that it occurred. A sight that would root the young man to the spot. From half-way down the office he saw something very familiar catch his eye. On the works noticeboard was a picture of himself with a red circle drawn around his head and a red arrow pointing to some writing. His story of how he had become a Christian and what it meant to him. Looking around the office he felt a million pairs of eyes staring at him. If the ground could have swallowed him whole he would have happily been its next course for dinner. If he could have climbed inside a filing cabinet he would have done so. But there was no place to hide, nowhere to run. What was he going to do? If you could die of embarrassment he would have died on the spot!

You might have guessed, Sam. The young man in the story was me. I felt so embarrassed that day. My church had printed a newsletter with my testimony on it. Somehow, someone at work had got hold of it and pinned it to the noticeboard for the whole world to see. I was sure I was going to be bombarded with questions and comments. By the time to go home no one had said a word. I walked out of the office with a huge smile on my face. It wasn't just relief! God had answered my prayers. I wanted to tell people at work that I was a Christian. God had told them all for me without me opening my mouth!

There are two points I want to share from that story. Firstly, God helped me to witness to people when I hadn't got a clue where to begin. Secondly, I felt so embarrassed. It wasn't the first occasion or the last. Why should this be the case? I don't know, because I do love God and I do try to love him. It's just that sometimes I find it hard to explain my faith or feel awkward. God <u>has</u> helped me to share my faith and when I do trust him and open my mouth I have been amazed at what has happened. So please don't despair. I think all Christians have had a similar experience to you, including me. I have enclosed a drama sketch and some Bible notes to try to help.

Yours, knowing what it feels like to fail,

Jake

Best friends, betrayal . . .
and a brand-new start!

Ever been let down by a friend? What about a best friend? If you have then you will know how dreadful it is. Someone you trusted has let you down. What now? Do you forgive and forget? Or do you finish the friendship? Which one would you choose?

Peter, the fisherman, was one of Jesus' best friends. Such a close and caring friend was he that when Jesus told his disciples that they would all leave him, Peter said not he. Peter's exact words were, 'Even if all fall away on account of you, I never will.' (Matthew 26:33)

Jesus replied, 'I tell you the truth, this very night, before the cock crows, you will disown me three times.' But Peter declared, 'Even if I have to die with you, I will never disown you.' (Matthew 26:34-35)

Strong words from a strong man. Powerful words from Peter. When the soldiers came to arrest Jesus, Peter was quick to take out his sword and fight. Jesus rebuked him. This was not the way. Jesus was arrested. The disciples fled. Peter with them.

In a cold courtyard before the break of day a man stood silently by the fire locked in his own thoughts. What was racing round his mind no one knew. He was silent. He was alone.

'This man was with him.' The words, like an arrow, sped towards Peter, hurtled into his heart.

'Woman, I don't know him.' The words fell from Peter's mouth and dropped like stones onto the ground, cold and hard.

'You certainly are one of them.' Another voice in the darkness cut deep into Peter's open wounds.

'Man, I am not!' Peter's voice was harsh now, strong and passionate, loud enough for all to hear.

'Certainly this fellow was with him, for he is a Galilean.'

His accent had given him away. His accusers were gathering around him – circling like vultures, as the grey light of dawn began to reveal the haggard features of Peter, the disciple. In one last desperate attempt to remove himself from this hideous night Peter cried out, 'I don't know what you're talking about!'

As Peter's voice cried in desperation it was met by the cries of a cock crowing. The three crows cut deeper than any sword into Peter's wounded heart.

Jesus turned and looked straight at Peter. Then Peter remembered the words the Lord had spoken to him. 'Before the cock crows today, you will disown me three times.' And he went outside and wept bitterly.

What a scene. What a situation. How would you have felt if you stood in Peter's shoes? What hope was there for you now?

Days later after the death and resurrection of Jesus, Peter meets his Lord once again face to face. It is a moving account of how Jesus reinstates Peter, how he shows him he loves him. (John 21:15-19)

We have a God of grace, of mercy, of love and of forgiveness. Sadly, we do fail him, we do let him down badly. The question is whether we look into his face again like Peter and utter those words, 'Lord, you know all things, you know that I love you.'

If we say and mean those words we will hear those two words spoken back, 'Follow me'.

Time to move on, to start again, begin afresh. We should never give up when God wants us to get up and follow him.

Do not . . . give up!

Message
To show people that even when we stumble and fall God will always be there to pick us up. We musn't become discouraged and give up.

Scene
Person 1 is sitting on the floor, head bowed, rubbing eyes. Person 2 runs past Person 1, suddenly stops, turns around and goes back, standing directly over Person 1.

P2   Are you all right?

A loud wailing noise comes from the person on the ground

P2   You don't sound all right.

More loud wailing

P2   Can I help?

Person 1 on the floor looks up, wipes their eyes then starts gesturing their arms frantically and trying to tell their story but it comes out in pitiful sobs

P1   Running along, I tripped, I tripped, fell and hurt my knee, my knee.

More sobs and wails. Person 2 looks at the knee

P2   I think I can see a scratch.

A loud cry from Person 1

P2   It's just a small scratch. So little you almost need a magnifying glass to see it . . . There's no blood.

More big sobs

P1   I fell down. I fell down again. I hate it, hate it, hate it.

All the time they are speaking they are stamping their feet on the ground

P2   Everyone falls down sometime.

P1   I do it a lot. Last week I tripped and fell head-first into a hedge.

P2   That must have hurt.

P1   Not at first it didn't.

P2   Oh!

P1   After two hours my head felt sore.

P2   Two hours!

P1   I couldn't get out. I was stuck. Next door's dog eventually found me and he dragged me out with his teeth. Another pair of shorts ruined.

P2   Sounds horrible.

P1   It was.

P2   I'll help you up. *(Holds out a hand)*

P1   No!

P2   No?

P1   No! No! No! I'm not getting up.

P2   Why not?

P1   Because.

P2   Because what?

P1   Because, because, because . . . that's why!

P2   You've got to get up.

P1   I'll fall down again.

P2   You might, everyone stumbles sometimes.

P1   But it hurts.

P2   But you can't just sit there for ever.

P1   I can, you watch me. I'll be here today. I'll be here tomorrow. I'll be here for ever.

P2   You'll get hungry.

P1   No I won't. I've just had my breakfast.

P2   Come on, or we'll both be late.

P1   I'm not getting up.

P2   School starts in a few minutes, you've got to get up.

P1   I'm not going.

P2   We're only five. Five year olds fall down a lot.

P1   How do you know?

P2   My dad told me.

P1   Oh.

P2   Come on.

P1   My leg hurts.

P2   I'll help you. *(Holds out hand. Person 1 on the floor looks up, thinks about it, then reaches out)*

Read John 21: 15-19

Q How do you think Peter might have been feeling when he met Jesus?
A

Q How did Jesus treat Peter?
A

Q Why do you think Jesus repeated himself three times?
A

Q How should we respond to God when we've failed him?
A

Q What advice would you give to Sam?
A

Any comments on what you've read:

Any questions you'd like to ask:

Unit 15

Putting faith into practice

Dear Jake,

I have been to the Christian Club at school! Let me announce it to the whole world: I HAVE BEEN TO THE CHRISTIAN CLUB AT SCHOOL!!

Your last letter really helped me. Thanks a lot. After my failure at school, remember with Eggo, I was feeling absolutely miserable. One minute I was wanting to tell the world about Jesus, the next minute I just wanted to crawl into a hole and disappear. What you showed me about Peter was so encouraging. How Jesus forgave him. But now I've said that word 'forgive', it reminds me of the main reason I'm writing this letter.

It all happened last Tuesday, the day when I finally plucked up the courage to walk down the corridor and actually go into the Christian Club. Once inside I really enjoyed it. The bloke who runs it, who all my mates think is sad, is a bit like you, Jake, not that you're sad! I mean he does the same kind of job as you. Once he did this really funny thing in assembly. I was dying to laugh but all my mates were looking spaced-out so I just put a lid on it. They think he's sad and call him names, but I don't. So where was I? Oh yeah, the Christian Club was good fun. They played a dead smart game, wrapped people up in toilet rolls, trying to make them look like Egyptian mummies. One girl was covered from head to toe, you ought to have seen her. It was hilarious. The man, Andy, went on to talk about the afterlife and what different people believed. He ended by saying how we can have eternal life through Jesus Christ. It was really good.

Walking home from school I was in a really good mood, despite the weather. It wasn't raining cats and dogs, it was raining elephants and camels. All day long the rain had been bouncing down. There was no one outside in the schoolyard at dinner time because the yard had suddenly turned into a swimming pool. Water was everywhere. One of the teachers tried to cross the yard and almost disappeared in a mass of water. You ought to have seen him. It was dead funny. Well, probably not that funny, not for him anyway, but I laughed . . . sorry.

I wished I hadn't laughed — not when things happened to me. Like I was saying, Jake, despite the rain I was walking home in a cheerful mood, even singing! I must have been singing quite loud because I never heard them coming. Never saw them until it was too late. One minute minding my own business, singing 'singing in the rain'. The next minute drenched from my socks to my school tie. I thought the shock was going to kill me, the water was freezing.

When I looked around I saw them. I saw them standing there, laughing like hyenas. Oh, they thought it was funny; they thought they were so clever. The ringleader was my brother, the rest were his so-called mates. Between them and me was a massive pool of water which they had thrown some bricks in, hence my rather wet and watery look. Even though I gave my brother my meanest scowl he still carried on laughing. If he laughed any more I seriously thought he would split his sides.

I was fuming. I didn't just see red, I saw every shade of red. One thing became clear . . . revenge, I had to have revenge. A part of my brain said no, a part of my brain informed me my brother was wearing his brand-new school clothes, the ones Mum and Dad had spent a fortune on, but the rest of my brain was yelling at me, do it, do it, throw the bricks, make him suffer!

The gang was laughing so hard they never even noticed what I was doing. Armed with a handful of bricks I hurled them towards my brother.

Splat! Splat! Splat! A hat-trick of perfect landings which completely soaked him.

He stopped laughing.

I legged it.

Locked in my bedroom (for safety) there was a loud knock on the door. I thought it was him but it was my dad.

'Go away. I am not here!'

'Samuel.'

Oh-oh, Dad must be cross, he's calling me Samuel.

'Samuel, I thought you were a Christian.'

I didn't know what to say so I said nothing.

'I thought you believed in forgiveness and turning the other cheek.'

How did Dad know that?

'Call yourself a Christian? You should practise what you preach.'

I felt ashamed.

Dad walked away.

Jake, how can I practise my faith when people, i.e. my brother, make life so hard for me?

Yours miserably,

Sam

Dear Sam,

Thanks for your last letter. I was really pleased, thrilled, delighted, tickled pink, over the moon. You can tell I was happy when you told me that you had been to the Christian Club at school. Standing up for your faith is so important. It always encourages me when I see young people piling through the door in the club I run at school. Well done, Sam! I would encourage you to keep on going now that you have made a start.

The rest of your letter was also very interesting! Oh brother! Some families do have them! I do know that family life can have its moments and that occasionally a wrong chord is struck in the harmonious day-to-day family life. In sympathising, Sam, I am not excusing, and from the tone of your letter I think I can tell how bad you feel. What is always good to remember is that we can be forgiven when we say sorry to God and really mean it. Sometimes we need to say sorry to people too.

We also need to be able to forgive others. Remember the Lord's Prayer? There is a part which says, 'Forgive us our debts, as we also have forgiven our debtors.'

Being forgiven is wonderful but we must also make sure that we practise forgiveness. I am not saying that it's easy, sometimes it can be extremely difficult, a real struggle we wrestle with. All I can say is God is good, God is gracious and he will help us in our struggles if we allow him to.

What your dad said is a real challenge to all Christians. Someone once said, 'If you talk the talk you have to walk the walk.' Sharing Jesus Christ is both verbal and non-verbal. Through what we say as well as what we do. The two should complement one another and go together like a hand in a glove. Enclosed are some notes. I do hope you find them of benefit.

Yours, an L-plate Christian,

Jake

Faith and deeds or dastardly behaviour?

The last hymn has been sung. The service books collected in. The vicar has shaken hands with everyone who has been in the Sunday meeting. Standing outside on the steps are two solitary figures. Both are regular attenders; they never miss a church service, they even have their own place to sit. One resides on a pew at the front near the font. One slinks onto a pew at the back near the sound system. They are the same age but there the similarities end. One is rich, bank accounts that run with lots of noughts in them. The other is penniless, surviving on scraps of social service handouts and whatever benefits exist. One changes their car like some people change their socks. One has holes in the soles of their shoes, the only pair they own. One has a wardrobe for every season of the year, bulging with the layers of clothes piled inside. One has the clothes he is wearing. They are standing on the steps in the chill of a winter morning. One of them shivers, the other ponders.

'This jacket has a mark on it.'

The man who is stamping his feet to try to keep warm takes a look. 'I can't see anything.'

'Look harder!'

With his teeth chattering and his body quivering he leans forward to further examine the clothing.

'There, man, look.' The gentleman with the fine coat pulls the gibbering, freezing fellow forward and points to the minutest speck on his garment.

'It's a crumb.'

'What!'

'I think it's a crumb.'

The rich man stares in disbelief.

'A crumb from the bread. You know, Communion.'

The light dawns and the wealthy man smiles as he flicks the morsel of food from his jacket. 'Still wish I'd worn something a bit warmer but that is the burden I have to bear.'

'Pardon?'

'So many coats to choose from, old man. Think yourself lucky you're spared such dilemmas. Good day.'

The man hunches up in his winter coat, smiles and disappears down the street.

The poor man blows into his hands trying to bring some warmth to his numb fingers, wondering what he will do for food that day.

What good is it, my brothers, if a man claims to have faith but has no deeds? Can such faith save him? Suppose a brother or a sister is without clothes and daily food. If one of you says to him, 'Go, I wish you well; keep warm and well fed,' but does nothing about his physical needs, what good is it? In the same way, faith by itself, if it is not accompanied by action, is dead.' James 2:14-17

What we believe must affect the way we live.

What we talk about must be what we live out in our daily lives.

Practising

A few questions to tax your brain . . .

- Do you think footballers practise?
- Do you think hockey players train?
- Do you think athletes go to the gym?
- Do you think anyone who wants to keep physically fit exercises?

I hope that you answered 'yes' to all of the above!

Perhaps they were obvious answers! Perhaps that is an understatement! But . . . what if footballers didn't practise? What if hockey players didn't train? What if athletes didn't go to the gym? What if people who wanted to be physically fit didn't exercise?

What would we have then? Players who were hopeless on the pitch, puffing for breath. Athletes who couldn't run a short distance, never mind a marathon.

We all know that those scenarios would not be allowed to happen. Neither for professional sports people, nor for people who are serious about their health.

The apostle Paul said this: 'Train yourself to be godly. For physical training is of some value, but godliness has value for all things, holding promise for both the present life and the life to come.' (1 Timothy 4:7b-8)

We need to put into practice our faith. We need to train ourselves to be godly. There is a discipline involved. There is a cost incurred. We must see that we have an important role to play in living our Christian life. Although God has given us his Spirit and the power for godly exercise, we still have a free will to exercise and choices to make.

Let us not be spiritually flabby but spiritually fit and ready for action.

Preferring

Before I was a Christian I used to play in a football team. I also used to captain and manage the side. Just before you start to say what a boasty-boy I am, let me give you a quick résumé of our team's results . . . It won't take long. We lost.

We didn't just lose but we lost big time, every time. As captain I tried to encourage my players to perform. My language was awful, my attitude appalling, my behaviour atrocious. When I became a Christian I stopped swearing; no one told me to – it simply ceased. I began to see my players as people, and treated them accordingly. Things changed and my team . . . still lost . . . big time. Did I like losing? No! Yet things had changed.

God helps all of us to change, to prefer his ways and not ours. To do what is right and not what is wrong. Isaiah says it better than I can:

'For my thoughts are not your thoughts, neither are your ways my ways,' declares the Lord. 'As the heavens are higher than the earth, so are my ways higher than your ways and my thoughts than your thoughts.' Isaiah 55:8-9

God's ways are always the best and when we become a Christian, God, the Holy Spirit, lives within us to help us to change, to give us the courage and the power to do so.

Perfecting

Put your hand up if you are perfect!

No hands?

Not a surprise. My hand didn't go up either. No human being is perfect. We need to practise our faith, train to be godly. But not one of us has made it to perfection . . . yet!

When we see him we shall be like him.

One day we will be like Jesus; one day we will be transformed. One day . . . when we meet him face to face we will be perfect – until then, train on!

Read James 1:19-27 and James 2:14-26

Q Why should we do more than merely *listen* to God's Word?
A

Q Why are faith AND deeds so important?
A

Q What stops us putting our faith into practice?
A

Q How can we overcome these obstacles?
A

Q What advice would you give to Sam?
A

Any comments on what you've read:

Any questions you'd like to ask:

Unit 16

Do I have talents?

Dear Jake,

Thanks for your letter. I am not perfect. I know I am not perfect. It is good to know that I am in excellent company with the rest of the world! Seriously though, I did take to heart what you said about practising your faith; you and James, the 'faith and deeds' man, remember? That story about the rich man and poor man was very striking. It really made me think.

I apologised to my brother. He pretended to faint. I apologised to my dad and he said he felt like fainting. I apologised to my mum and she did faint!

You could say they were slightly shocked and surprised by my actions. I think they were secretly happy. I know I was. It was like a huge weight being lifted from my shoulders. Mum must have been really impressed or something because later the same day she came and had a chat with me.

'Samuel?'

'Yes, Mum?'

'I've been thinking.'

'Yes, Mum?'

'Would you like to go to church tomorrow?'

'Yeah! How come? Which one? I mean, not the one with the lady with the . . . '

Mum began to turn beetroot red.

'No, no, of course, Mum, not <u>that</u> one I mean, but where?'

Mum told me how she had bumped into an old friend shopping at the local supermarket. She hadn't seen her friend for years, at school she was one of the most miserable people in class but now her face was beaming. 'She looked like a lighthouse,' Mum said. Mum always has funny ways of describing people.

Mum noticed that her friend was wearing a cross. Anyway, to cut Mum's conversations short, they got chatting and her friend told her she was a Christian now, how God has really helped her and she was part of a great church. The rest, as they say, is history.

The next day, Sunday morning, we were off to church. Mum even let me wear my jeans. She said it's the inside that really counts, as long as I'd washed behind my ears. She does have a funny way of saying things!

This church was different. They had a band! Guitars and drums and things. People clapped, some waved their hands in the air, some people were dancing. Nearly everyone was smiling and seemed really happy to be there. During one of the quiet songs I saw mum rubbing her eyes. I asked her if she was all right and she said, 'Don't be silly, I'm at home.' She does have a funny way of saying things.

They guy who preached was really good. He made me laugh a lot too. What he said was both encouraging and challenging. He was talking about gifts, saying God had gifted each one of us. I agreed with what he said but thought, 'Not me'. I have no gifts. My art teacher told me I can't even draw a straight line with a ruler. It sounds good God giving us gifts, but where are mine? How can I use what I don't have? I'm not saying he's lying, I'm just struggling to think of anything I'm any good at.

Any ideas on the gifts front, Jake?

Yours,

clueless, giftless and feeling sorry for himself,

Sam

Dear Sam,

Thanks for your letter. I was so glad to read about you going to church with your mum, especially when you both really enjoyed it. That is excellent. I do hope you can settle there. It is so important to find a good church, somewhere you can belong, be cared for, and somewhere you can be spiritually nurtured and fed. It also needs to be a group that you can give something to, because your contribution is vital. Remember the team?

Talking about contribution reminds me of the reason why you wrote your letter. What you asked was a really good question; your questions always are!

I have enclosed some notes and a sketch. I do hope they are helpful.

Yours, to a gifted friend,

Jake

Digging for treasure

Faded writing on crumpled parchment. Your eyes struggle to discern the words, your mind struggles to comprehend the information.

A treasure map.

You have been given an ancient treasure map and told that all you have to do is follow it to find riches galore. Of course you would like to believe it, but really, a treasure map!

Walking across the room you pull open a chest of drawers and stick the map deep inside. Something inside you prevents you from throwing it away or destroying it but you are not going to be foolish enough to do anything with it.

Weeks roll by, months come and go, the years begin to fly. Still stashed in a drawer in your living room is a treasure map. Still in the recess of your mind lingers the thought 'What if?'. 'What if it was real?', 'What if it was true?', 'What if you wasted your whole life never discovering the truth of the buried treasure?'

The drawer creaks open, your hands fumble for the map. Piles of paper are dislodged as the search becomes desperate in its intensity and uncertainty. Where is the treasure map? Which drawer was it? Who could have removed it? Where could it possibly be?

Sitting on the floor you feel a cold sweat. Have you missed out on the greatest treasure you could have found? Have you been a fool? Thoughts begin to assail you as you sit and wonder.

One last search. One last attempt before the day draws to an end and your hopes disappear with the sunset. Your fingers carefully remove every scrap of paper laid across the bottom of the drawer. Your eyes scan every sheet, every piece that is unearthed.

The treasure map.

It has not been lost. It has been waiting all along. You hold it in your hands in triumph. You look at that faded writing once again and know that it is time to go looking; it is time to begin the search; it is time to dig for treasure.

The nagging thought begins to drip like an annoying tap. What if it is all a hoax? What if it is all a waste of time? The edges of the map curl in your hands. Decision time.

What about the treasure in your life? I am not talking about silver or gold but something far more precious: your God-given gifts and abilities. Some people's talents are obvious and lie on the surface: an outstanding mind, a pair of legs that carry you like the wind, a razor-sharp intellect or muscles the size of Popeye's. Some people's physical, mental and practical skills stand out like a sore thumb. From the moment they can crawl you can tell, well almost! For others, perhaps the majority of the population, gifts and talents do not appear so clear. Do we have any? Are we prepared to dig for treasure? Will there be anything of value to unearth? Does everyone have something wonderful to contribute? Is there a treasure map to our talents?

Yes there is. It is another ancient document, yet as fresh and relevant as the day the ink dried. The Bible points the way forward, shows and teaches us God's plans and purposes for us. Let's open the treasure map and discover the truth.

Before I formed you in the womb I knew you, before you were born I set you apart; I appointed you as a prophet to the nations. Jeremiah 1:5

For we are God's workmanship, created in Christ Jesus to do good works, which God prepared in advance for us to do. Ephesians 2:10

There are different kinds of gifts, but the same Spirit. There are different kinds of service, but the same Lord. There are different kinds of working, but the same God works all of them in all men. 1 Corinthians 12:4-6

What amazing thoughts!

God has individual plans for each one of us. Different gifts, different service, but all from God himself.

How to discover your gifts . . . or tips on how to shovel . . .

There, beneath the earth's surface, lie untold treasures. In your hand is a shovel, the equipment required. All you have to do is bend your back and begin to dig. Physical effort is what is needed. What are you going to do?

Dig! Dig! Dig! That's what you should do. Dig until you find it. The same principle applies with discovering your spiritual gifting.

Here a few pieces of practical advice.

1 Be willing to serve. Gifting isn't about showing off, its about using what you have for the benefit of others.

2 Ask people you trust what they think about your talents/areas of gifting. Sound out people who can give sound honest advice.

3 Don't be frightened to have a go at something, even if you feel nervous or if you fail.

4 Ask people to pray for you to find out what God wants you to do.

5 Have a strong desire to please God because he is the one who has blessed you with life and all your talents and he only wants to bless you and do you good.

Read Matthew 25:14-30

Q How many of the servants were given talents?
A

Q What does the parable teach us about what we should do with our talents?
A

Q How will God view our burying of our talents?
A

Q How important is the quantity of talents we have?
A

Q What advice would you give Sam?
A

Any comments on what you've read:

Any questions you'd like to ask:

Unit 17

Be encouraged and be an encourager!

Dear Jake,

I followed your advice. Oh boy, did I follow your advice. Reading your letter cheered me up and made me think, 'Yeah, God's good, he's probably given me some really smart gifts – when I find them!'

Last Sunday at church I decided to take any opportunity that came my way. No matter what it was, I was going to give it a go. So here, Jake, for your benefit and amusement, is what happened.

The guy who was leading the service gave out the notices as well. One of them made me sit up and think, 'Yeah, that's me.' What he said was this:

'Next week we are organising a team of people to help move Mrs Finkle's possessions to her new home. We are planning to do this on Saturday so hopefully a number of people can help. Many hands make light work . . . It's not in the Bible . . .'

Lots of people laughed when he said that.

'. . . but it does make sense. There will be light refreshments served at Mrs Finkle's new abode as long as there aren't too many hands, if you know what I mean!'

More laughter.

A good number of hands went up in the air. Mine was the first. Mum looked shocked; it's a good job she was sitting down or she could have fainted again.

After the service I had to put my name down on a sheet of paper and was given an address and a map how to get there. Receiving the map reminded me of your story. Now I was going to unearth my gift of 'Super Sam the removal man.'

Saturday came around and I was on my way to Mrs Finkle's. Mum had given me a packed lunch to take, with some chocolate cake inside.

'That's to share,' she said.

'Yeah, sure, Mum,' I thought to myself. Mum's home-made chocolate cake is the best in town. There was no way anyone else was going to get their slobbering choppers on it. Surely God doesn't want us to share our chocolate cake with people? Can't we have our cake and eat it?

Arriving at Number 5, Cawthorne Avenue, I thought I was looking through a telescope. Mrs Finkle's house was massive; it was larger than large. Standing in her driveway were four vans and a gigantic removal van the size of which I had never clapped eyes on before. There were so many people milling about they looked like ants, it was incredible.

'They don't need me,' I reasoned.

I was just about to turn tail and run when I heard a shrill 'Yoo-hoo, yoo-hoo, is that Samuel I can see?'

I turned and gave a weak little smile.

'Your mother told me all about you.'

I could feel myself blushing from the tips of my toes to the roots of my hair. 'Really?' I said through clenched teeth.

'Come on, Samuel, you can help with my china.'

At first I thought she meant China – as in the country! Looking at the house, I thought it was big but not that big! Everything went smoothly at the house. I moved a few vases, tea cups, pots and pans, the odd ornament or two and then jumped in one of the vans to be transported to Mrs Finkle's new 'humble abode' as she described it. A small village was more accurate a description.

Inside her palatial home, everyone worked like beavers. No one stopped working as all the vans were unloaded and possessions placed inside.

'Who wants to help put my grand piano in the first-floor music room?'

My head said, 'Not on your life!'

My heart said, 'Yes!'

My hand was in the air, volunteering once again. Mrs Finkle looked delighted as a group of men gathered around the grand piano and began to lift.

The first step was fine. No problem. Stealing a glance up the stairs I tried to calculate how many steps to climb, problem was the stairs disappeared around a corner and just kept going.

I was young, I was fit, I was healthy, I was strong, I was out of breath and shattered after five steps. My back felt like a giant hand was ripping it out of its sockets. Do backs have sockets? My fingers felt like they were being turned into pulp. My chest was wheezing, my arms were aching, my legs were buckling and that's why . . . I let go.

I didn't think everyone else would! Honest! For some reason when my side went down and I accidentally toppled into the man next to me and he let go, the people pulling at the top didn't want to carry it any more. I don't know why but they didn't.

We flung ourselves out of the way as the piano careered down the flight of stairs. For a grand piano the sound it made wasn't very tuneful. As it lay as firewood at the bottom of the steps all eyes trained themselves on me but before anyone could utter a word I was out of there. Down the stairs, through the front door and legging it all the way home.

I didn't say a word to Mum and told her I felt too sick to go to church, which was true.

Jake, help!!

Yours,
pulling muscles in every part of his body,

Sam

Dear Sam,

Have you ever seen the film 'Casablanca'? Remember the line 'Play it again, Sam'? Oh boy, oh boy, oh boy, whatever next? I can only appreciate how you are feeling and I do sympathise. What you need to know is that whatever happens, accident or not, God loves you. It might sound a simple thing to say but it is totally radical. The God of the whole universe who hung the stars out in space cares about your aching back, your injured feelings and your emotional turmoil. He sees, he knows and he cares. God, who made the vast universe in which we take up residence is a God who is close to you.

Sam, I hope my words are words of encouragement that you take to heart because they are true. Encouragement is so important, especially when you need it. To emphasise the message I've slipped in a few notes for your personal help.

Yours,

hoping to stay in tune (tee-hee), sorry, in touch,

Jake

Encouragement in times of fear, failure and feeling fed up!

He who has never failed is he who has never tried, never got up out of bed in a morning, never risen onto his hind legs and walked into the day with all that it has to offer. If you know what failure feels like then join the club with the rest of humanity, we are all members.

Perhaps it is a school exam, or breaking a friend's confidence. Perhaps it is keeping an appointment or losing at marbles. Perhaps it is in not keeping a promise or in forgetting to feed next-door's cat whilst they are on holiday. Whatever the circumstances, however big the calamity, whichever way the cookie has crumbled, failure is something we all encounter, all have to endure. How we can be enabled to cope and to carry on is through encouragement. Someone to come alongside us when life is dire and we are full of disappointment. Someone to sit by us in our anxieties and our anguish. Someone to hear our voice of derision and reason with us when we are stuck firmly in the doldrums.

Rejoice with those who rejoice; mourn with those who mourn.
Romans 12:15

We need to lend more than a sympathetic ear: we need to lend our emotions, we need to care. Genuine heartfelt concern that carries us beyond the boundaries of our own life and into the territory of someone else's. Where does this heartfelt desire come from? Which well brings out this life-refreshing water? Well, there is only one place to look.

If I speak in the tongues of men and of angels, but have not love, I am only a resounding gong or a clanging cymbal. If I have the gift of prophecy and can fathom all mysteries and all knowledge, and if I have a faith that can move mountains, but have not love, I am nothing. If I give all I possess to the poor and surrender my body to the flames, but have not love, I gain nothing. Love is patient, love is kind. It does not boast, it is not proud. It is not easily angered, it keeps no record of wrongs. Love does not delight in evil but rejoices with the truth. It always protects, always trusts, always hopes, always perseveres. Love never fails. 1 Corinthians 13:1-8

Where does this wonderful love originate?
God is love. 1 John 4:8

What is to be our motivation?
For Christ's love compels us. 2 Corinthians 5:14

Why did Jesus come into this world?
For God so loved the world that he gave his one and only Son. John 3:16

I hope the message is ringing loud and clear. When we go through dark times we need the light of God to shine upon us. That light can come through you and me.

You are the Light of the world. Matthew 5:14

Encouragement . . . practical, verbal and helpful!

Understanding that we all need encouragement is one thing. Desiring to help people is another, but what about giving it? Or in other words, how do we pick someone up when they are flat on the floor? If this was in a physical sense then it wouldn't be too difficult. Someone is sprawled across the pavement, they are moaning and groaning, stretching and reaching out with their hands. All you have to do is stick you arms out and help them up.

What about when the needs are emotional? What if the pain is a deep-seated root of inadequacy or a feeling of being unloved? What kind of encouragement can we offer to the brokenhearted? Pious words and spiritual posturing will not help the poor person whose poison runs deep on the inside of the arteries of their heart. So where do we begin?

Words.

'Sticks and stones may break my bones but names can never hurt me.'

You've probably heard those words in the children's playground. Possibly used them yourself! What they tell us is a partial truth. Sticks and stones do hurt; we can all vouch for that, especially if we have bruises to show! The second part of the rhyme is so misleading, so inaccurate, so . . . wrong. Name-calling does hurt. Like graffiti upon our soul, words are sprayed from a can of filth and poison. I know, I can remember words spoken to me from my early years. What about you?

'You'll never be any good.'

'You were not wanted.'

'I hate you.'

'You're horrible.'

Sometimes words spoken in the heat of the moment are words that sting and can leave a nasty mark.

Here's what the wisdom book, Proverbs, tells us about words.

He who guards his mouth and his tongue keeps himself from calamity. Proverbs 21:23

A wise man's heart guides his mouth, and his lips promote instruction. Proverbs 16:33

Pleasant words are a honeycomb, sweet to the soul and healing to the bones. Proverbs 16:24

A fool's mouth is his undoing, and his lips are a snare to his soul. Proverbs 18:7

The tongue has the power of life and death, and those who love it will eat its fruit. Proverbs 18:21

Powerful words from Proverbs and a last few words on words from the Book of Ephesians.

Do not let any unwholesome talk come out of your mouths, but only what is helpful for building others up according to their needs, that it may benefit those who listen. Ephesians 4:29

When words are not enough . . .

Words are important. Words are powerful. Words can bless and words can curse, but sometimes, to help people and encourage them, we need to do more than speak, we need to act.

If someone is hungry, they need feeding. If someone is cold, they need clothing. If someone is hurting, they need helping. There are some wonderful organisations set up to be practical in caring for others – love in action. But what about on a local level? What about on an individual basis?

Sometimes needs are obvious, especially physical ones. A wheelchair that needs pushing, shopping that needs carrying, a garden that needs digging. Sometimes needs are not so obvious: a person who always seems to be alone, a person in pain who keeps it inside, a heart that hurts but cannot be seen.

How can we help?

- Be sensitive and aware of the people around you.
- Be prayerful.
- Be prepared to get your hands dirty.
- Be on the lookout for local charities and concerns.
- Be caring.

Whatever you do, be helpful

Be practical, not patronising. Be positive, not nitpicking, Be proactive, not pious. Whatever we do, we need to do something. To encourage someone, to help put courage into them, to be a shoulder to lean on. Each of us has a responsibility to be a friend to rely on, giving those around us strength to carry on.

Sam,
   Just a few more things before I get this in the post . . .
   Here are a few more verses on encouragement for you to
chew over:

'. . . encourage one another daily, as long as it is called Today,
so that none of you may be hardened by sin's deceitfulness.'
Hebrews 3:13

'And let us consider how we may spur one another on towards
love and good deeds. Let us not give up meeting together, as
some are in the habit of doing, but let us encourage one
another – and all the more as you see the Day approaching.'
Hebrews 10: 24-25

   Sam, be encouraged . . . and, Sam, be an encourager!
   Your friend,

   Jake

   PS Thanks for the encouragement that you are to me.
   PPS Remember confession.
   PPPS Remember Mrs Finkle . . .

Read Romans 12:9-21

Q How should we love?

A

Q Where does love come from?

A

Q In what practical ways can we care for people?

A

Q How can we be encouragers to others?

A

Q What advice would you give to Sam?

A

Any comments on what you've read:

Any questions you'd like to ask:

Unit 18

Dealing with temptation

Dear Jake,

What a week! Everything (and I mean everything!) has happened this week. I don't know where to begin, so I probably best start at the beginning! Hope that makes sense.

It was Sunday night, the day after Mrs Finkle's tinkling piano became timber. I had stayed in my bedroom all day and was still there when there was a knock on the door. 'No reason to panic,' I said as my heart sent thumping messages to my brain. I heard Mum go to the door and then the voice.

'Yoo-hoo, it's me!'

The hairs on the back of my neck curled (some people's stand on end, mine curl). I was hoping Mum would shut the door or say I was asleep or that I had mysteriously vanished off the earth but all she said was, 'He's upstairs, I'll just go and get him.'

Mum!

Despite my attempt to hide under my bed, Mum found me and dragged me out. 'What's the matter with you, Samuel? That nice lady from church is here. She probably wants to thank you for helping her move.'

Then she said it. 'I'm so proud of you, Sam.' There was a tear in her eye and there was a crocodile in my throat (a frog is way too small to describe how I felt).

When I got to the top of the stairs I could see Mrs Finkle's head. She looked up when she heard me and . . . smiled! She actually smiled. I thought someone must have dropped a china vase on her head or something! She was grinning, a lopsided curling smile that stretched from ear to ear. Whatever state her mind was in, I knew I had to explain what happened, calmly and rationally.

'I'm sorry, I'm sorry, I'm sorry. I am so sorry. I feel bad, I feel awful, I feel terrible, I feel lousy, I feel sick, I have been sick many times. I'll pay you back every penny even if it takes till

I get my OAP bus pass. I will give you everything I have. I will come and work in your village, I mean house, every weekend. I'll dig the house, I mean garden. I'll do whatever.

Whilst my mouth was working on overtime, Mrs Finkle's was just grinning.

'Samuel,' she shrilled. 'It's all all right.'

My mouth stopped open in mid-flow.

'I needed a new piano. It's fully insured. I know it was an accident. I heard all about it. I should never have let you carry it up those stairs. It was all my silly fault. You've been so kind and generous, coming to help me move and leaving that delicious chocolate cake for us to devour.'

'Rats!' I thought. I left the cake!

'I can only imagine how you felt. So please, Samuel, let us put the incident behind us. We all make mistakes. Even Hilda Finkle.'

Her smile was still stuck in place and I could feel myself breaking out from a cold sweat into a big grin.

Next day at school I was on a real high. Talk about forgiveness, talk about encouragement, Mrs Finkle is a real gem.

Perhaps it was because of the mood I was in or perhaps it was because it was the last week of term but whatever the reason I got myself into an awkward situation.

Eggo (remember him?) spotted me at break and called me over. Why he couldn't come and speak to me I have no idea. Eggo was lurking by the big school bins and wearing a pair of dark shades even though we haven't had any sun for weeks!

'Here, Sammy boy, a ticket.' Eggo never gives you anything.

'What's the cost?'

'To you, Sammy, my mate, my buddy, my best pal?'

'Yeah.'

'A tenner.'

'Ten quid?'

'Bright lad, Sammy, got it in one. I take cash, cheques, credit cards . . .'

'How can you take credit cards?'

'Don't ask, Sammy.'

'What's it for?'

'Ronny's Rave, Friday night.'

Ronny's Rave, the dodgiest night club in town was legendary. As long as you were tall enough to open the door they would let you in. What went off inside was rumoured all over school.

'Special night, Friday. End of term, a lot of stuff going down at Ronny's.' Eggo lowered his sunglasses onto the bridge of his nose and gave me a 'you know what I mean' look.

'Paying now or later?'

I stared at him.

'You are coming — the whole year is going. You don't want to be the odd one out, do you?'

I didn't know what to say. A part of me wanted to go but something else was saying no. I could feel a game of tug of war starting in my mind.

'See you later, Eggo.'

'Think about it, Sammy. You know it makes sense.'

He pushed his sunglasses back up his nose and started to chew, only he didn't have any gum!

Jake, help!

Yours, confusedly and worriedly,

Sam

Dear Sam,

What a week! You were quite right! First, Mrs Finkle's graciousness and kindness, and then the encounter by the bins with Eggo. What a week . . . and what to do? I think you may guess, Sam, what my advice would be. A simple answer: 'no'. No, don't do it. No, don't go. No, stay as far away as you possibly can. You will only live to regret it. Yet it is easy for me to say that, miles away and without the pressure and temptation you are facing. We all face such struggles in life. Every one of us. To try to help I have enclosed a story, a sketch and some notes.

Yours, praying you make the 'right' choice,

Jake

Pressured, playing and paddling

A few years ago I went to Scotland. Not on holiday but to an outdoor pursuits centre with a group of fellow youth workers. The weekend had been good fun and on the last morning we were taken to a loch for a spot of canoeing.

I do not canoe.

My wife mastered the simple technique of how to handle the paddle whilst I was stood on the shore receiving one-to-one personal tuition from the instructor. All eyes watched me struggle. All mouths laughed in my direction. Eventually the instructor released me to join my friends. Time to canoe.

Some went fast. Some raced across the loch. I took the scenic route. Round and around my little canoe spun just so I could take in all the beautiful Scottish scenery. By the time I arrived at the far side of the loch they were all ready to set off back.

Once again I was the last person to arrive, but what concerned me wasn't my late arrival but our destination. We were well short of the shoreline with all the canoes lined up in a row. Alarm bells began to ring inside my head. Something was wrong, something was not good about this scenario. When the instructor opened his mouth he had a huge grin plastered on his face. That confirmed my suspicions.

'We are going to play a little game.'

My worst fears were realised when he explained the rules of his 'little game'.

Rule 1: Stand up in your canoe

Rule 2: Climb out of your canoe

Rule 3: Run across everyone's canoes

Rule 4: Run back

Rule 5: Sit down in your own canoe

My rule: Do not play silly little games with canoes.

Splash after splash after splash after splash. No one made it. It was impossible. It was silly. It was my name that was now being chanted.

'Jake! Jake! Jake! Jake!'

Nothing was going to budge me.

'Jake! Jake! Jake! Jake!'

Not peer pressure, not anything.

'Jake! Jake! Jake!'

I was out of my seat and moving but before I could even attempt to cross the canoes, before I could even stand up, I slid in slow-motion style to the end of my canoe and 'plopped' into the water. Not even a 'splash' simply a 'plop'!

What was really embarrassing was that I wouldn't even climb back into my canoe and the instructor had to pull me to shore whilst I doggy paddled and held on tightly to the back of his boat!

Tempting, turning, trusting

Whatever age we are, whatever stage of life we are at, we all face temptation. It may be through peer pressure, or our own selfish nature, but we all have to deal with temptation.

> *I do not understand what I do. For what I want to do, I do not do, but what I hate, I do.* Romans 7:15

The apostle Paul knew the struggle too. There is a battle within us.

> *For the sinful nature desires what is contrary to the Spirit, and the Spirit what is contrary to the sinful nature.* Galatians 5:17

Even as Christians, even with God's Holy Spirit to help us, we still face temptation and pulls to go in the opposite direction. The question is, can we cope with them, overcome them?

The short answer is Yes! Here briefly is how.

> *For God did not give us a spirit of timidity, but a spirit of power, of love and of self-discipline.* 1 Timothy 1:7

> *In all these things, we are more than conquerors through him who loved us.* Romans 8:37

God has given us the power. The question is, 'Have we chosen to go to God for his help?' Do we want to turn to him?

We thank God for Jesus, our Saviour, the one who died on a cross, to take the punishment for our sins, but do we know him as our Lord? The one who is in control of our life? The one whose ways we choose to follow, no matter what we feel like doing? Jesus is not someone to lord it over us but he wants to rule in a righteous way because all he does is good and right.

In facing temptation, in turning away from what is wrong, in trusting in God, can we be safe, can we be secure, can we be strong?

For I am convinced that neither death nor life,
neither angels nor demons,
neither the present nor the future,
nor any powers,
neither height nor depth,
nor anything else in all creation,
will be able to separate us
from the love of God
that is in Christ Jesus our Lord.
Romans 8:38-39

Drive on!

A sketch to explore Jesus being the Lord of our lives.

Scene
Two people are walking towards a car. One of them goes to the driver's door and stops in his tracks . . .

One Sorry, force of habit.

    Both of them smile, swap places, with the other person climbing into the driver's seat. Once seated the driver looks over

Two I can't start the car.

One You can't?

Two No.

One I thought you said you were a good driver. I thought you were supposed to be the best. My friends recommended you. I can't believe this! What a waste of . . .

Two I can't start the car without the car key.

One Ah . . .

Two You do have it?

One Yes.

Two And you do want me to drive?

Pause

One I did ask you to drive.

Two I know. That's why I'm here.

One I want you to drive.

Two Could I have the car key please? *(Pause)* You still want me to drive, don't you?

One After my performance, of course I do. Three speeding fines, one smashed headlight, two broken mirrors, four flat tyres, five old ladies scared to death on the pedestrian crossing as I crossed at the same time, six parking tickets, seven passengers now on tranquillisers, eight close shaves, nine cats' lives taken, ten times knocking over next-door's garden gnomes, eleven times running out of petrol on the motorway, and twelve times bumping into Mrs Simpson's dog.

Two Not to forget the partridge in a pear tree.

One Pardon?

Two Twelve days of Christmas?

One A joke?

Two Sorry.

One Here's the key.

Two What are you doing?

One Just checking that it's in neutral.

Two I do know what the gears are for.

One What's that?

Two First.

One That?

Two Second.

One That?

Two Third. And the other one is fourth, and over there is reverse. Now may I start the car?

One Sorry. I'm just not used to someone else driving my car.

Two If you would like to . . .

One No, no, no, you drive. Drive on.

The key is turned in the ignition and the engine started

One I think you're going too fast.

Two We haven't set off yet!

One Well, your foot seems very heavy on the revs.

Two Does it?

One Maybe not that heavy. Maybe just enough to start the car.

Two Thank you.

One Drive on.

Two Why have you got hold of my hand?

One You must be very careful with the handbrake.

Two I will.

One Very, very gentle. You must release it very carefully.

Two Would you like to . . .

One No, no, sorry. Please, drive on.

Two You have very long legs.

One I have?

Two Not many people could reach the brake pedal from the passenger seat.

One Oh, I suppose you would like me to remove my foot from the brake?

Two Only if you want me to drive.

One I do. Please. Drive on.

The engine revs.

Two We nearly hit your gate post!

One I thought you said you were a good driver!

Two Well, I normally drive with only my hands on the wheel.

One Oh.

Two Not with the passenger's hands as well.

One Oh.

Two Do you want me to drive?

One You were going to turn right?

Two Yes.

One I always turn left.

Two Not today.

One But I always go the other way!

Two Not if I'm driving.

One Can't we both drive?

Two Both holding the wheel?

One Yes.

Two No.

One Oh.

Two You asked me to drive. Now please . . . do you want me to drive or not?

Dear Sam,
   As I write this, the sun is shining, I am with my family at our favourite coffee house, and I am looking forward to the rest of summer . . . and especially the camps – only three weeks to go! See you there.
   God bless, God keep you, God loves you to bits.
   Yours, a fellow follower,
   Jake

Read Luke 14:25-34

Q What does Jesus mean by 'carrying his cross'? [verse 27]
A

Q What are the costs involved in being a Christian?
A

Q What does it mean to call Jesus 'Lord'?
A

Q Why is it worth everything to follow Jesus?
A

Q What advice would you give to Sam?
A

Any comments on what you've read:

Any questions you'd like to ask: